PASHA MARLOWE, MFT

Creating Cultures of Neuroinclusion

A Framework for Peopling and Engaging Neurodiverse Talent

First published by Neurobelonging 2024

Copyright © 2024 by Pasha Marlowe, MFT

All rights reserved. No part of this publication may be reproduced, stored or transmitted in any form or by any means, electronic, mechanical, photocopying, recording, scanning, or otherwise without written permission from the publisher. It is illegal to copy this book, post it to a website, or distribute it by any other means without permission.

First edition

ISBN: 979-8-9919909-0-5

Editing by Charlotte Montemayor
Typesetting by Charlotte Montemayor

This book was professionally typeset on Reedsy. Find out more at reedsy.com

I want to give a shout out to every queer, disabled, and neurodivergent person who faced internal and external resistance and still chose to bravely express their truths, claim their worth, and live a more aligned life.
I am inspired and humbled by you all.

Contents

Preface — iii
Acknowledgments — iv

I   Part One

1   Neuroinclusion is Peopling Done Right — 3
2   Neurodiversity is About Everyone — 8
3   The Business Case For Neuroinclusion — 13
4   From Policy To Action — 15
5   Prepare For Gen Z And Rainbows — 17
6   Language As A Catalyst for Change — 19
7   The Neurodiversity Paradigm — 21
8   The Expansive Neurodivergent Umbrella — 25
9   Identity-First or Person-First Language — 29
10 Neurodiversity-Affirming Language — 32
11 Neurodiversity-Affirming Practices — 38
12 Functioning Labels — 44
13 Apparent and Non-Apparent Disabilities — 46
14 Social vs. Medical Model of Disability — 50
15 Superpower or Disability? Yes, And. — 53
16 Accessibility Best Practices — 58
17 Neuroinclusive Policies — 62
18 Inclusive Design — 66
19 Access and Support Needs — 69
20 Barriers to Neuroinclusion — 72
21 Strengths-Based Approach — 76

22	Accountability	78
23	Intersectionality	80
24	Neurodiversity/LGBTQIA+ Affirming	83
25	Leading Neurodiverse Teams	85
26	Respect Rubric	89
27	Framework Summarized	92
28	Trailblazers and Resources	94

II Part Two

29	Neuroinclusion Framework Summary	101
30	Glossary of Terms	103

III Part Three

Afterword	107
About the Author	108

Preface

Imagine a world where all kinds of people have an equitable
opportunity to thrive.
Imagine a world where people are cared for,
simply because they are human.
Imagine a world where access and support needs
are accommodated.
Imagine a world where everyone has
inherent value and agency.
Imagine a world of liberation, freedom, and peace.

– Pasha Marlowe

Acknowledgments

Thank you to every one of my individual, couples, and group clients that I have seen over the past 32 years. You trusted me to hold space for your most intimate thoughts and relationships and allowed me into your hearts. It has been an honor.

Please know that I have enjoyed working with each and every one of you. I wake up excited every day to co-collaborate with you and help you create the lives you desire and deserve.

To the neurodiversity advocates and educators that came before me, thank you for building the bridge as you crossed it and trailblazing paths towards neuroinclusion. The world is a kinder, more inclusive, and accessible place because of the work you do.

To the leaders who read this book and implement neuroinclusive policies and strategies, thank you. You are making a difference on an individual, team, organizational, community, and societal level by choosing to embrace neurodiversity and accessibility. Pave the way. Show other leaders and organizations how neuroinclusion is beneficial for business and imperative for humanity.

Thank you to my business and life coach, Mel Robbins, who said my neurodiversity-affirming work is critical and encouraged me to become a professional speaker for greater impact. Thank you, Impact Eleven, for creating an incredible community of speakers and thought leaders that inspire me daily.

Thank you, Daine, Sarah H., and Sarah M. for being the bestest friends ever. Every time I wanted to give up, you were all there, cheering me on and reminding me of my impact and worth.

Thank you, Char, for rescuing me and this book in the final hours with extraordinary patience and kindness.

Thank you, John, for supporting my work, keeping the dogs as quiet as possible, and offering me space to think and write. I'd say I am done writing for a while and can do more laundry now, but I would be lying. I have many more books in me. Sorry, not sorry.

Thank you, Josh and Emi, for loving and supporting me throughout each of my transformations.

And, Little Bear, you know you are my heart. When you and I were experiencing our darkest hours, my purpose on this planet came into the light. Witnessing your bravery to keep choosing your life, empowered me to reclaim my own. I wish it didn't take 50 years to finally release my neurotypical, straight, people pleasing masks, but without your love, I would still be stuck behind them, instead of here, standing strong and visible as a neuroqueer advocate and second time author. Go, us!

I

Part One

1

Neuroinclusion is Peopling Done Right

We as a society need to people better. That is, we need to care about humans better.

I think we can all agree that transformation is needed and that the status quo, both in and out of work spaces, is not working in service to all humans. Creating cultures of neuroinclusion can be the catalyst for the change we wish to see, where all people, no matter their differences, have an opportunity to thrive at work and beyond. For too long, neurodiversity, disability, and accessibility have been left out of DEI strategies. Not anymore.

In this book I will be using "people" and "peopling" as verbs, as in "when we people, we relate as equals" and "peopling well leads to increased engagement at work".

Peopling is about how we relate to and interact with each other. Peopling is about how we connect and communicate with other humans around the world. For the sake of this book, we will be talking about peopling in the workplace and how creating cultures of neuroinclusion is the path to enthusiastic engagement and sustained enthusiasm for work. If we are going to work, we want to feel aligned, and ideally passionate, we spend our time and the people we spend time with.

You can absolutely take these same concepts of peopling and creating cultures of neuroinclusion out of the workplace and into your homes, schools, and communities. This is a framework for universally caring for others and honoring unique frames of reference.

You have probably experienced the word peopling in a lighthearted context about the exhaustion of navigating social interactions, as in "I am done peopling for the day." As a neurodivergent, sensitive, and empathetic person, I resonate with that concept. Peopling well can be exhausting because it requires presence and energy.

I propose we elevate the term peopling to mean the practice of caring for people well, which is not a casual concept, but something we can all improve upon and is serious business.

Speaking of business, learning how to people IS the essential skill needed for success in any business that involves people, which is every business on the planet. When people are cared for and respected, they stay.

When people are mistreated or undervalued, they leave. If we want to create an inclusive and healthy workplace culture where people are fully engaged and motivated to work, we need to get peopling right.

Here is my working definition of peopling: Peopling is the practice of caring for people with respect and kindness, affirming identities, supporting access needs, valuing unique and authentic ways of functioning, and holding empathetic space for differences and opposing views.

Sounds like a description of an impactful leader, doesn't it?

I agree, but I also want to emphasize that ANYONE, no matter their role, can be a change agent, anyone can help transform a culture, and anyone can help enhance engagement and practice the art of peopling. I believe every person should feel valued and have the opportunity to thrive so they can live and work to their full potential and empower others to do the same.

As a therapist, coach, and advocate, I have over three decades of professional peopling experience. I have learned much about how people think and feel. I have learned about how people hurt and how people love. I have worked with thousands of people around the world and, universally, I find people want to be cared for better and appreciated more. I have yet to meet a person who does not want to be treated with kindness and respect. I have yet to meet a person who does not want to be believed, valued, and supported. No matter their lived experiences and intersecting identities, every person I have ever met wants agency and freedom.

It is through this lens of peopling, intersectionality, and agency that I came to the compassionate work of neuroinclusion. Neuroinclusion is the practice of including everyone, neurodivergent and neurotypical alike. It is about specifically creating an environment that values and accommodates different neurological functioning styles.

This includes different ways of moving, relating, feeling, thinking, and learning. While we will absolutely talk about neurodiversity, neurodivergence, and disability, I want to be clear that neuroinclusion is about a diversity of bodies and minds working and collaborating together in harmony. Like neurodiversity and peopling, neuroinclusion is about all of us. No one is left out of this conversation.

This is not a book about specific neurotypes (such as ADHD and autism), nor a book on how to manage specific types of people. Rather, it is a framework for creating inclusive, flexible, and collaborative workplaces where each employee's unique needs are considered and everyone has an equitable opportunity to thrive. Neuroinclusion requires paradigm shifts about diversity and differences. It is about assuming less and listening more.

For a visual representation of the Neuroinclusion Framework refer to the back of this book, in Part Two. To download a printable copy that you can keep handy (or hand out), go to my website www.pashamarlowe.com.

You might be wondering why it is necessary to create cultures of neuroinclusion, rather than just inclusion. Doesn't inclusion mean including everyone? Yes and no. Yes, in theory, and no, in practice-certainly not in the current practice of most workplaces. General inclusion initiatives often neglect to strategize for the specific support needs of neurodivergent and disabled people.

As with other justice movements, the neurodiversity movement seeks civil rights, equality, respect, and full societal inclusion for neurodivergent people. Until neurodiversity, accessibility, and disability are fully reflected in DEI policies and strategies or until all minds and bodies are actually supported, talking about neuroinclusion is imperative.

We need to raise awareness about neurodiversity and disability. We need to increase our willingness to work and connect with all kinds of people, even those with different functioning styles.

We need a framework for creating cultures of neuroinclusion, where every mind and body is included and valued. We need a framework for how to people, especially when we don't understand or agree with the people we are communicating with. We need inclusive language to help us navigate these challenging conversations with respect. We need training and professional development on these concept sand space to practice the art of peopling.

In collaborating with organizations around the world, I find the keys to expansive and sustained engagement are when people feel non-performatively cared for, included, valued, respected, and recognized. Barriers to engagement that bring enthusiasm to a halt include negative or performative work culture, ineffective communication and leadership, limited career opportunities, inadequate recognition, reduced flexibility and autonomy, and lack of psychological safety.

When people feel safe and free to bring their whole selves and all of their intersecting identities to work without fear of negative consequences, they can innovate, problem solve, and collaborate. When people feel like they need to conceal an identity or mask their authentic selves, they will disengage and explore other spaces that will accommodate and celebrate all that they are.

This book is an actionable framework for creating cultures of neuroinclusion, where peopling, proactive inclusive design, and accessibility are top priorities.

The following framework will benefit anyone who cares about culture transformation and inclusion at work. It is a global guide for peopling, a practice that will ensure an enthusiastically engaged and motivated workforce. It is a manual for leaders, DEIA advocates, HR professionals, consultants, and coaches. I hope it also validates, affirms, and empowers neurodivergent, disabled, and LGBTQIA+ folks to recognize their strengths, challenges, and claim their access and support needs.

Mostly, I hope anyone who engages with this book comes to think and feel about differences differently and considers becoming an ally and advocate for neuroinclusion.

2

Neurodiversity is About Everyone

The most frequent piece of feedback I receive after facilitating workshops about neuroinclusion is "Wow! I had no idea how much I misunderstood the concept of neurodiversity and how impactful it is in the workplace." Perhaps this will be your experience as well. I invite you to remain curious, lean into learning and unlearning, and open your heart to the world of differences.

Once I fully understood the concept of neurodiversity, it changed how I saw myself and others. It changed how I talked about myself and others. I became a more compassionate and empathetic person. I learned how to people and make connections on a deeper level.

I see differences differently now. Everywhere I go, I notice how neurodiversity influences the way people interact with themselves, each other, and the world. Neurodiversity is endlessly fascinating, and I am so glad that differences are finally receiving the spotlight they deserve.

Over the next few chapters, we are going to explore paradigm shifts that may make you question everything you ever learned about neurodivergence, disability, and even mental health. It may feel disruptive.

I hope so.

We need disruption to change the way we work and lead, especially in order to meet the needs of younger generations who seek work that feels aligned with their passion and purpose.

Gen Z, in particular, enthusiastically engages in workplaces where diversity and differences are celebrated. We have to be more proactively inclusive at work than ever before. We have to adapt the way we talk about ourselves and others. We have to get to the root of stigma and biases. We have to think about differences differently. We have to create systemic change, from the top down and the bottom up. Our society and workplace is ready for this transformative and paradigm shifting conversation.

Let's get into it.

Individuals Are Not Diverse

Let's start with a common misconception. Neuro doesn't mean brain-it means nervous system, which includes the brain. Neurodiversity is not only about diversity of thought, no matter what search engines say.

Neurodiversity is the diversity of human minds and nervous systems and infinite variations of functioning and feeling. Neurodiversity is not a trait or something an individual can possess. It is a fact of nature.

The human species is neurodiverse. Individuals are not neurodiverse, just as individuals cannot be diverse. Diversity requires more than one thing and "diverse" refers to two or more people who are different from one another. Diverse is not defined as a person or people who are different from you, as if you are the "norm" and they are "diverse."

Do not use the word "diverse" to refer to people who are, for example, not white, not heterosexual, or not disabled. Be specific and say what you mean. It is far more inclusive, effective, and accurate to use clear and unambiguous language. Say Black, Indigenous, Hispanic, Asian, Middle Eastern, and other people of color. Say LGBTQIA+ or queer. Say disabled. Rather than saying a person is neurodiverse, say neurodivergent.

Neurodivergent is an identity used by individuals whose neurobiology diverges from neuronormativity, or society's idea of what is "normal," "right," or "ideal." Neuronormative expectations vary, depending on culture. Neurodivergence encompasses how people think, learn, feel, act, move, and love.

It is a holistic and whole person term about how one embodies neurodivergence. Neurodivergent people choose this identity and are empowered by the word. Use it.

The Neurodiversity Movement

Neurodiversity is a biological fact. The neurodiversity movement is a sociopolitical and activist movement that seeks civil rights, equality, respect, and full societal inclusion for neurodivergent people. The neurodiversity paradigm is a perspective on neurodiversity as well as a philosophical foundation for the neurodiversity movement (I expand on the neurodiversity paradigm in Chapter 7).

Neurodiversity impacts every interaction each of us has with other people in the world. In order to practice effective peopling, we have to embrace the idea that there are a wide variety of neurotypes and ways to function in the world. Saying someone's functioning is "normal," "right," or "ideal" is a value judgment statement. As the neurodiversity paradigm states, there is no one "normal" style of functioning, just as there is no "normal" ethnicity or gender.

Embracing the idea that there are infinite ways of thinking, learning, feeling, communicating, moving, and functioning is the path to inclusion, specifically neuroinclusion.

Neuroinclusion As A Competitive Advantage

There is plenty of research proving that increased diversity of all kinds makes for a more successful and profitable business. Higher levels of diversity are correlated with increased innovation, problem solving, productivity, adaptability, and collaboration.

And, yet, most organizations have not fully embraced the multitude of ways their talent is already diverse, nor have they expanded their hiring practices or DEI strategies to include neurodiversity or accessibility. Those that do are certainly enjoying the competitive advantage.

Word is spreading like wildfire as to which organizations are making non-performative efforts to create cultures of neuroinclusion. Many organizations say they are "neurodiversity-affirming," without strategies to back it up.

Saying you are neurodiversity-affirming in policy is not helpful if you are not neurodiversity-affirming in practice or support systems.

Likewise, a neurodiversity-hiring program is useless and possibly exploitive if there is no support system for neurodivergent people. Furthermore, if a neurodiversity-hiring program is actually an autistic hiring program (as so many are), you are marketing and recruiting on false pretenses and will end up excluding and angering the very people you intended to include.

Be specific. Say what you mean and then do what you say. Action and accountability matter. Organizations that understand how to affirm, support, elevate, and include all neurodivergent people are not only more likely able to retain their talent, they will create a long-term loyal workforce.

From Creating to Cultivating Cultures of Neuroinclusion

And while a few organizations are attempting to create cultures of neuroinclusion and establish neurodiversity hiring programs, I witness few that are cultivating cultures of neuroinclusion. By cultivating, I mean nurturing the culture, such as providing ongoing training around neurodiversity, disability, and accessibility or providing extra mental health care.

Efforts have to extend beyond hiring and retaining practices and expand to strategies for neurodiverse employees(that's all of them) to collaborate together (neurodivergent and neurotypical alike). Everyone needs to be invited to the table and ensured that their voice and experiences matter. The benefits on a business and human scale when this is done well are profound.

3

The Business Case For Neuroinclusion

I know, return on investment (ROI) matters. What can organizations gain from creating and cultivating cultures of neuroinclusion? How does being neuroinclusive and peopling better make businesses money?

Two words: engagement and retention.

All the research shows that any efforts to create a more diverse and inclusive workforce benefit the bottom line. Diversity and inclusion leads to increased innovation, problem solving, productivity, adaptability, collaboration, and psychological safety. When there is enthusiastic engagement, organizations avoid stagnation, turnover, and unnecessary conflict.

Fulfilled and cared for talent makes for a successful and profitable business. But wait! There's more!

Let's play and do this ROI of DEI exploration "infomercial" style...

When you invest in cultures of neuroinclusion, you will enjoy higher levels of engagement, loyalty, and brand respect. A US Dept of Labor analysis found that organizations who embraced neuroinclusion and implemented neurodiversity-affirming practices saw a 90% increase in employee retention.

90%! But that's not all!

If you create cultures of neuroinclusion, you also enjoy less stigma, biases, microaggressions, and bullying - the Roots of most interpersonal conflicts and cultural problems at work.

And BONUS!

If you act now and proactively create cultures of neuroinclusion today, the younger generations who are mindfully seeking neurodiversity-affirming places to work, will flock to you and rave on social media that you are an organization that ACTUALLY gets it!

I'll even throw in an extra surprise gift for you! Future children and grandchildren will thank you for being on the right side of history. Your legacy will be as a neuroinclusive trailblazer!

OK. OK. This marks the end of my infomercial metaphor. Thanks for playing the ROI of DEI game, better known as diversity and inclusion efforts make you money when you do it right.

4

From Policy To Action

You WILL attract and retain a diversely talented workforce if you do the work of neuroinclusion. Even if your organization is not (yet) strong in DEIABJ policies and strategies, this framework will help. What does DEIABJ stand for, you may be wondering? Here's a review:

- **D**-Diversity
- **E**-Equity
- **I**-Inclusion
- **A**-Accessibility
- **B**-Belonging
- **J**-Justice

Every one of those letters matter. I have seen this acronym take many forms with the letters in different positions (IDEA, JEDI, DEIA, DEIB). I believe each of these letters has a place in our conversation about how to people better and create cultural transformation. Not surprisingly, I do not agree with recent efforts to defund DEI and de-center equity (D&I).

I am disheartened every time the "A" for accessibility is left out of the acronym or conversation altogether. What good are any efforts and initiatives if they aren't accessible?

In order to survive and thrive in the future of work, given all we know about incoming generations and what they care about, all organizations need to put the concepts behind all of these letters into action.

The workforce is evolving rapidly. Be prepared for more diversity than ever before-specifically more cultural and ethnic diversity, neurodiversity, disability, and queerness than ever before. I will be using "queer" as an umbrella term for LGBTQIA+ and recognize that some LGBTQIA+ people do not prefer "queer." Queer is how I identify and the term I am most comfortable with, but my apologies if it offends anyone.

Know that you simply cannot be neurodiversity-affirming without also being LGBTQIA+ and gender-affirming. The correlations between these communities are strong, especially for the younger generations.

Many people identify as both neurodivergent and queer-some use the term neuroqueer. The neuroqueer wave is growing and will rise high in 2030, when 38% of the workforce is Gen Z, and they will be actively seeking neuroinclusive spaces. The framework I share in this book will help you future-proof your organization.

If you put all these letters, DEIABJ and LGBTQIA+, into action, you will experience enthusiastic engagement and talent that will sing your praises.

5

Prepare For Gen Z And Rainbows

Why is understanding and embracing neuroinclusion especially important now?

By 2025, Generation Z will account for about 27% of the total workforce. By 2030, the numbers rise to 38% of the workforce, making the attraction, retention, and engagement of young talent crucial. While there has been some progress on neuroinclusion and disability inclusion, as evidenced by the sixfold growth in corporate disability policies and programs, neurodivergent and disabled talent remains largely underrepresented. For example, 80% of educated autistic people are unemployed. That's stigma and stereotyping glaring at us in the face, friends.

This is one of my favorite and most impactful statistics: according to a recent study by Zen Business, half of Gen Z and a third of millennials identify as neurodivergent and disabled. Disabled includes apparent and non-apparent disabilities, such as neurodivergence and mental health. In many ways, the world and society is becoming more disabling.

Climate change, a challenged economy, gun violence, socio-political conflicts, ongoing residual trauma from the pandemic, and a decrease in trust in authority, systems, and institutions, contribute to this dynamic.

All of this comes at a time when organizations and educational institutions are struggling more than ever to attract, retain, and engage new talent.

Gen Z is not only the most diverse generation we have seen in the workforce— it is also the most entrepreneurial! It will become more and more challenging for any organization to attract younger talent, especially if they aren't willing to honor, accommodate, and celebrate differences.

The workplace is becoming more queer every year as well. Each generation identifies more with neurodivergence, disability, and queerness than the generations that came before it. The LGBTQIA+ community doubles with each generation. As of this publication, 30% of Gen Z identifies as LGBTQIA+, whereas only 15% of millennials and 5% of Gen X identify.

I expect all of these numbers to rise significantly within the next few years. I always say-prepare for more rainbows!

Not everyone is excited about more rainbows, I understand. Stigma, biases, and discrimination make it challenging to find non-performative, accessible, and inclusive work spaces. For example, disabled people are sometimes hired so organizations can "check the diversity box." These same organizations may offer no support systems to accommodate access needs. When this happens, disabled people attempt to work in an inaccessible environment, but ultimately feel too overwhelmed, too burnt out, and too disrespected to thrive. It's not if they will leave inaccessible jobs, it is when. Note that the cost of turnover is significantly more than the cost of supporting the talent you already have!

Fun fact: Most accommodations cost $0-$500. Accessibility is not the complicated and costly venture some make it out to be. We will explore inclusive design more later but know that the accommodations you offer people with access needs end up benefiting everyone.

6

Language As A Catalyst for Change

As we set out on our journey to create cultures of neuroinclusion, we must understand the power of language. The words we choose shape our perceptions, influence our actions, and ultimately define our organizational culture. In this rapidly evolving landscape of diversity and inclusion, language is not just a tool for communication—it is a catalyst for change. Inclusive language can transform cultures.

Neurodiversity and disability are complex, multifaceted concepts that have been historically misunderstood and misrepresented. Let's unpack important terms, challenge outdated paradigms, and set a foundation of today's most accurate and inclusive language.

When we use accurate and inclusive language, we signal respect, demonstrate understanding, and create spaces where everyone feels valued and heard. Conversely, outdated or insensitive language and euphemisms can create barriers, reinforce stereotypes, and alienate the very talent we aim to attract and retain.

We will explore key definitions, examine the nuances between apparent and non-apparent disabilities, discuss identity-first versus person-first language,and tackle the complexities of destigmatizing our vocabulary. We will challenge the notion of "normal" and embrace the rich tapestry of human neurocognitive variations.

Language is ever evolving. What is considered appropriate today may change tomorrow. My aim is not to provide a static rule book, but to equip you with the understanding and flexibility to navigate this dynamic landscape with empathy and respect.

I do not speak for all neurodivergent, disabled, and queer people. I highly value agency and believe every person should get to determine how they identify, the words they use, and what their support and access needs are. When possible, Ask The Person (ATP) and do not make assumptions about their identity or the language they prefer to use.

In our efforts to cultivate and nurture neuroinclusive cultures, this awareness and flexibility in language use is not just about political correctness, it's about demonstrating genuine respect and understanding for the diverse experiences and identities within our organizations.

7

The Neurodiversity Paradigm

Let's explore the necessary paradigm shift away from the current pathology paradigm and towards the neurodiversity paradigm. This, in and of itself, is disruptive, as therapists and doctors are still trained in the pathology paradigm. When we challenge mental health paradigms, we challenge the diagnostic statistics manual (DSM), which is currently the therapist's guide for who gets diagnosed and with which label.

Which leads to an important question: why do most diagnostic labels of human experiences and challenges end in "disorder"? Disordered according to who and as compared to what "ideal"?

Shifting From the Pathology Paradigm to the Neurodiversity Paradigm

The concept of neurodiversity represents a significant shift in how we view and understand neurological differences. Traditionally, variations in neurological function were viewed through a pathology paradigm—a medical model that categorized these differences as disorders or deficits.

The neurodiversity paradigm, in contrast, recognizes and celebrates neurological differences as a natural part of human diversity.

Under the neurodiversity paradigm, we understand that the human mind can respond in various ways, each mind unique with its own strengths and challenges. This perspective doesn't deny the very real struggles that some individuals face, but it re-frames these challenges as differences rather than deficits.

This shift from a deficit-based model to a strength-based model is transformative. It allows us to focus on individuals' strengths and unique perspectives rather than solely on challenges or perceived limitations.

While the pathology paradigm asks, "What are we going to do with all these people who are different and don't fit into society?," the neurodiversity paradigm asks "What are we going to do about our society that does not accommodate people with differences well-yet?"

I always add "yet," because I am hopeful and optimistic and believe, with awareness and a desire to make our world a more beautiful place, this paradigm shift is possible-even in medical and mental health systems that are born out of the pathology paradigm.

To use my experience in the mental health system as an example, I was trained as a therapist 32 years ago and was taught to use the Diagnostic Statistics Manual (DSM) to diagnose and determine who is "disordered" and who is not, which in turn, determined who would receive treatment, medication, and insurance coverage and who would not.

As a systems thinker, it never felt accurate or fair to determine a person "disordered" or "a problem to be fixed." I see things systemically and recognize patterns of interaction and everyone's responsibility in creating oppressive systems of power and privilege. But truth be told, it wasn't until I hit 50 and menopause that I had the courage to speak up against the DSM and the pathology paradigm to my mental health colleagues.

Becoming an advocate and an ally means you may lose people, but you gain integrity. I knew the pathology paradigm did not align with my values or the way I think about people. I stepped away from the world of traditional therapy for a long time and am finally starting to see a shift in the mental health field away from the language of "disorders" and towards differences.

The conversation around the root of the pathology paradigm is endlessly fascinating and angering and will not fit in the space of this mini book. However, I do believe the exploration of understanding how capitalism, patriarchy, colonialism, communism, and white supremacy created the pathology paradigm, is worthy. For the deep dive, I recommend my friend Sonny Jane Wise's thought-provoking book, *We Are All Neurodiverse*.

Drop the "D"

Neurodivergent is an identity, not a diagnosis. People who identify as neurodivergent reject the label"disorder." They focus on differences as neutral, not value judgments, and explore strengths rather than deficits. Rejecting the label "disorder" does not deny challenges or even disabilities. A neurodivergent person may have high support and access needs and consider themselves disabled and still reject the labels "disorder" or "deficit."

If someone receives a diagnosis of ADHD, an unfortunate label with "disorder" and "deficit" baked in, they still do not have to identify as "disordered."The diagnostic label does not make it true.Each person has the agency and right to decide how they wish to identify and describe themselves.

Autistic advocate, professor, and author of *Neuroqueer Heresies*, Dr. Nick Walker, explains, "If you reject the fundamental premises of the pathology paradigm, and accept the premises of the neurodiversity paradigm, then it turns out that you don't have a disorder after all."

How would we think and talk differently about ourselves and others if we dropped "disorder" from our language? Would people feel less broken if they saw themselves as simply different? Absolutely!

My call to immediate action is for us all to DROP THE "D"! Anytime you hear a label with "disorder" at the end, drop it. For example, rather than autism spectrum disorder, simply say autism. Rather than bipolar disorder, simply say bipolar. You get the idea.

8

The Expansive Neurodivergent Umbrella

Neurodivergence describes any neurofunctioning that diverges from neuronormativity, or society's idea of what is "normal" or "ideal." Neurodivergence can be innate (such as autism), developed (such as anxiety), or acquired (such as traumatic brain injury). Neurodivergent is not a diagnosis, it is an identity that people choose. It is an identity that should be believed, respected, and supported.

Ask The Person (ATP)

It is important to not make assumptions. Always Ask The Person (ATP) how they wish to identify and what their access and support needs are.

Some neurodivergent people consider themselves disabled and some do not. Some neurodivergent people consider their nuances "superpowers" and some feel that terminology disregards the challenges of being neurodivergent. It is up to each person to determine how they identify and describe their experiences.

Many neurodivergent people define their neurodivergence as a core part of who they are, not something they would ever want to fix, cure, or treat.

Rather, they may choose to manage their experiences or celebrate them. Notice I did not say symptoms, conditions, or traits. Those terms imply pathology, so I support using experiences and differences, especially until we understand how the individual identifies and defines their needs.

ADHD/VAST

Attention Deficit Hyperactivity Disorder (ADHD) has the pathologizing terms "deficit" and "disorder" in the label itself. Even "hyperactivity" can be seen as a value judgment. For this reason, I will use VAST alongside ADHD in this book. VAST stands for Variable Attention Stimulus Trait and was coined by Drs. Edward Hallowell and John J. Ratey in their book ADHD 2.0. The term VAST is intended to be more accurate and less stigmatizing than ADHD and highlights unique abilities rather than deficits. Because VAST is less widely known, I will note ADHD/VAST to avoid confusion.

AI is Sometimes Wrong

Currently, the narrative of neurodivergence in our society, including what most AI, search engines, and statistics describe, is inaccurate, incomplete, and potentially harmful. A limited or uninformed source may say neurodivergent is synonymous with:

- Autism
- ADHD/VAST
- Dyslexia
- Dyscalculia
- Tourette's (notice I dropped "Syndrome")
- Synesthesia
- Acquired brain differences (e.g., from injury or illness, such as TBI)

The "neurodivergent umbrella" includes all of the above, plus...

- Mental health experiences listed in the DSM (Diagnostic Statistics Manual)
- Anxiety, depression, bipolar, PTSD
- Epilepsy
- Down syndrome (some refer to Down Syndrome as chromosomal diversity)
- Chronic health issues (ex: neurological effects of Lyme or mold toxicity)
- LGBTQIA+ identities (more on this later; when you diverge from the performance of neuronormativity, you are likely to diverge from hetero and cisnormativity which are inherently intertwined. NOT all neurodivergent people are queer, but I may argue all queer people are neurodivergent)

And more, as neurodivergent includes any functioning that diverges from neuronormativity

20% Neurodivergent? I Think Not.

Given the expansive definition and awareness of the neurodivergent umbrella, it is clear that the popular statistics showing that 20% of people are neurodivergent are wildly underestimated.

Mental health challenges are on the rise. Furthermore, the statistics of 20% are inaccurate because many people choose not to disclose their neurodivergence or are even aware they can identify as neurodivergent.

From my lived and professional experience, I would guess the prevalence of neurodivergence to be closer to 75%. Neurodivergent is not a medical term or diagnosis, but an identity for people who diverge from neuronormativity.

When I present the neurodivergent umbrella to organizations, a common declaration I hear from audience members is "Oh! Well, in that case, I am neurodivergent, too! I had no idea what that word encompassed"! As our understanding and recognition of neurodivergence increases, so will the percentage of people who identify.

More people are not "becoming" ADHD or autistic, for example. We have always been here. But more people are understanding neurodivergence and identifying as neurodivergent. Thus, the workforce is becoming more neurodivergent by the day.

9

Identity-First or Person-First Language

Two primary approaches have emerged in the area of inclusive language around neurodiversity and disability: identity-first language and person-first language. Understanding these approaches and their implications is key to respectful and inclusive communication.

Person-First Language

Person-first language puts the person before the disability or condition. For example:

- "Person with autism" instead of "autistic person"
- "Individual with a disability" instead of "disabled individual"
- "Someone who has dyslexia" instead of "dyslexic person"

The rationale behind person-first language is to emphasize the individual's humanity first, suggesting that their disability or neurodivergence doesn't define them. This approach aims to separate the person from their condition, highlighting that they are more than their disability or neurodivergence. Many neurodivergent people prefer person-first language, especially with acquired neurodivergences, such as with PTSD or brain injuries.

Identity-First Language

Identity-first language, on the other hand, puts the disability or neurodivergent identity first. For example:

- "Autistic person" instead of "person with autism"
- "Disabled individual" instead of "individual with a disability"
- "Dyslexic student" instead of "student who has dyslexia"

This approach is based on the idea that disability or neurodivergence is an integral part of a person's identity much like race, gender, or nationality. Proponents of identity-first language argue that it promotes disability pride and rejects the implication that disability is something negative that should be separated from the person.

I find more often than not that people with innate forms of neurodivergence, such as ADHD/VAST and autism, prefer identity-first language as it feels less pathologizing and stigmatizing.

Agency and Autonomy in Language Choice

The key is to respect individual preferences, agency, and the autonomy of each person to decide how they want to be addressed. The Ask The Person (ATP) concept can not be overstated: always ask the person how they wish to identify and what language they prefer to use.

Best Practices for Inclusive Language around Identity:

- Ask and Listen: When in doubt, the best approach is to ask individuals how they prefer to be addressed. Listen to their preference and respect it.
- Be Consistent: Once you know someone's preference, use it consistently in your communications about or with them.
- Be Flexible: Understand that preferences can vary not just between

individuals, but also within communities. What works for one autistic person might not work for another.
- Context Matters: In some situations, particularly in legal or medical contexts, person-first language might be required. Be aware of these contexts while still advocating for individual preferences where possible.
- Educate Others: Share your knowledge about these language considerations with colleagues to foster a more inclusive environment.
- Evolve: Language and preferences evolve over time. Stay informed about changes in preferred terminology within different communities.
- Prioritize Respect: Above all, approach all interactions with respect and a willingness to learn and adapt.

The goal of using either person-first or identity-first language is the same: to communicate respectfully and inclusively. By being mindful of these language considerations and respecting individual preferences, we can create environments where everyone feels valued, understood, and accurately represented.

10

Neurodiversity-Affirming Language

Neurodiversity-affirming is a way of thinking that embraces natural neurological differences and views them as strengths, rather than deficits. Neurodiversity-affirming professionals and spaces should be validating and empowering.

Neurodiversity-affirming people believe that:

- Differences in how people function, think, feel, and relate to others makes each person unique and makes the world more interesting
- Every mind and body is equally worthy and valuable
- Disabilities resulting from neurological differences are rooted in societal barriers, not individual deficits.
- Neurodivergent is an identity, not a diagnosis, and is a term created to reject the idea of people being "disordered" or needing to be "fixed," "cured," or "treated."

But what good is it to be neurodiversity-affirming if we do not have neurodiversity-affirming practices or neuroinclusive policies?

What Should We Actually Say?

Let us discuss some day-to-day examples of how we can talk to and about our neurodivergent selves, loved ones, and coworkers.

I hear often that people do not include or talk to people who are different from them because they worry that they will offend or say the wrong thing. Trust me when I say it is far better to try, far better to include, far better to engage than to avoid, exclude, and disengage. Silence and avoidance are microaggressions and can be quite harmful to the very people you are trying to keep from harm.

Be a curious, humble, and empathetic leader. Be prepared to learn and unlearn. Get comfortable with getting it wrong and trying again until you get it right. Know better, do better.

Do Not Make Assumptions

Remember Ask The Person (ATP) how they identify and what their access and support needs are. Do not make assumptions based on other neurodivergent or disabled people you know.

There is a saying, "You've met one autistic person, you have met one autistic person." You can replace autism with literally any neurotype, neurodivergent or neurotypical. We are all different and have nuanced needs and desires and unique preferences.

It is always respectful to focus on the individual's lived experiences rather than a diagnosis, and certainly rather than deficits or assumptions. Be strength based and strength focused when possible. If not, be neutral with your language.

Challenge Neurotypical Expectations

We have to challenge our own societal views as to what professionalism looks like. A highly competent, productive, and professional neurodivergent person may struggle with social situations, eye contact, over-stimulating environments, or neurotypical ways of functioning. A neurodivergent person may not dress, move, or speak the way society says is "professional." They may even be non-verbal. None of this speaks to their abilities to complete their work.

Time and time again I hear from leaders how they "grossly underestimated" their neurodivergent talent. Match strengths and skills with tasks and projects and you will see any employee thrive. Assume competency, but also assume there will be support needs. One does not negate the other. Help them succeed and you both win.

"This is Simple" and "Will Just Take A Minute"

Please, please, please stop putting time estimations on tasks, emails, and posts. Saying "this form will take 30 seconds to fill out" or "take 2 minutes to complete the assignment" or "this is a simple task" is ableist and does not take into account learning differences or disabilities that make it more challenging to access information according to neurotypical standards and expectations.

Similarly, notice how much you say "just," as in "just look at this for a second" or "just fill this out" and recognize the ableism. For some people, a seemingly simple task is incredibly challenging. For many ADHD/VAST folks, for example, "easy" things are really hard and "hard" things are surprisingly easy.

It's a paradox—sometimes a superpower and sometimes a disability.

Use Accurate Language

Say disability. It is not a bad word. Disabled people don't avoid it, so why should non-disabled people? Euphemisms like "differently-abled," "diffability," or "special" might make the non-disabled person more comfortable, but it dismisses the lived experience and challenges of the disabled person. Say disability.

Similarly, autism is not a bad word. There is no need to say "on the spectrum" if the person has identified as autistic. Remember that neurodivergent is NOT synonymous with autism and encompasses many neurodivergences under the neurodivergent umbrella.

While we are at it, mental health is not taboo. "Mental health challenges" or "issues" is not wrong to say. I would avoid "mental illness" and certainly avoid words like "crazy." I know you don't mean harm by throwing the word "crazy" around. Consider impact versus intent.

There Are No Diverse or Neurodiverse Individuals

There are no neurodiverse individuals! I still see this phrase used all too often, even from educators and neurodiversity educators. Let us use accurate language. Neurodiverse is not synonymous with neurodivergent, nor is it a kinder way to say neurodivergent. Neurodivergent is the accurate term.

Saying "diverse individuals" is inaccurate and offensive, as there are no diverse people. You need more than one person for diversity to exist. And say what you mean. Don't say spectrum if you mean autism and don't say diverse if you mean Black. Many of these terms are rooted in racism and ableism.

Many Black, Brown, and Indigenous neurodivergent people have expressed that terms like "neurospicy" are offensive and rooted in racism. I know many people will disagree with me here, since neurospicy is fun to say and I keep saying ATP, but if a group of people is explaining why a word is offensive, I think it is best to avoid using it.

Value agency and want people to have the freedom to describe themselves however they wish without negative consequences. People who are educating others on the language of neurodiversity should be extra cautious and aware of terms that are non-inclusive and offensive to many.

A Brief Note on Tone

The global workforce is diverse in a multitude of ways, including language. It is important to recognize how intersectional identities influence language (syntax, grammar, structure, etc.) and culture. Sometimes in communication with neurodivergent people, specifically autistic people, there is conflict around tone.

For example, an autistic person is likely to be honest, specific, and accurate when giving feedback. Often, this is received as "harsh" or "combative"- even more so when added bias around race and ethnicity is at play. The listener can become defensive and shut down, perhaps even forget what the topic of conversation was about and turn the attention to the way something was said.

Some autistic people have difficulty regulating the tone of their voice and are often told they are "too loud," "too quiet," or "flat." This dynamic is complicated further if people do not speak the same primary language, are non-verbal, or have different neurotypes (see the "double empathy" section below). The key is to focus more on the words people express and less the tone in which they say it.

The "Double Empathy Problem"

The "Double Empathy Problem," a term coined in 2012 by Dr. Damian Milton in his studies of communication differences between autistic people and non-autistic people, explains that people of different experiences struggle to understand or empathize with each other. Milton's theory challenges the idea that autistic people lack empathy and suggests that autistic people simply express emotions differently, which makes it difficult for non-autistic people to understand them.

This "double empathy problem" challenge holds true in communication between any people who are different from one another, not just autistic people and non-autistic people.

Similar challenges exist when people communicate from different cultures or languages. It makes sense that people with different neurotypes and experiences struggle to communicate effectively. The "problem" is that the person whose neurotype is seen as the minority is the one who is often described as having "communication issues."Rather than recognizing the differences in neurotypes, language, or culture, there is a focus on deficits and difficulties.

When talking to people of a different neurotype, just as you would in talking to someone from a different culture, be aware of your biases and avoid stereotypes and assumptions. Ask for clarification as needed.

Presume competence and good intent.

Recognize the intersecting identities at play and keep an open mind to learning about different ways of communication and functioning.

11

Neurodiversity-Affirming Practices

Here is a reminder on the working definition of peopling:

> Peopling is the practice of caring for people with respect and kindness, affirming identities, supporting access needs, valuing unique and authentic ways of functioning, and holding empathetic space for differences and opposing views.

We are far from this more beautiful world. But every day we get closer, and now you are part of the cultural transformation we need to see!

Peopling in Practice

Neurodiversity is about all of us. It is not just about hiring, retaining, and supporting neurodivergent people. No! The work of neuroinclusion is about creating cultures where ALL minds and bodies can work and live together in harmony. It is about creating a world where, no matter how people function, all people are treated respectfully and equitably, and everyone has an opportunity to thrive. It's about a world where the practice of peopling is valued and prioritized. Practice is the key word there.

Peopling is something that we have to practice every day in every interaction with others.

Top 10 Neurodiversity-Affirming Practices

Being neurodiversity-affirming is not useful if you do not take action and implement neurodiversity practices. These are some practices that affirm, accommodate, advocate, align, and hold people accountable:

1. Challenge stigma, biases, and assumptions.
2. Hold people accountable when you witness micro-aggressions, bullying, or discrimination.
3. Offer accommodations and environments to support access and support needs.
4. Value agency and believe people when they share their identities and needs.
5. Center intersectionality, equity, respect, and transparency.
6. Foster and model an inclusive and accepting environment for all minds and bodies.
7. Stay informed about the current inclusive language of neurodiversity and disability.
8. Shift focus from perceived deficits to unique strengths, perspectives, and preferences.
9. "Nothing about us, without us," especially when determining new policies and strategies.
10. Practice and prioritize peopling.

Lived Experience

The "experts" on neurodivergence and disability are not always those with advanced degrees, books, and experience talking on stages. Nor are the experts only people with formal diagnoses (remember how diagnosis and disclosure intersect with privilege).

The real experts are those with lived experience as neurodivergent and disabled people. They don't just talk, they know. Honor and believe lived experience. Invite people with lived experience to the decision tables.

Sensory Challenges and Needs

When creating neurodiversity-affirming spaces and experiences, it is important to prioritize sensory challenges and needs. I have yet to have a conversation with a person (not just neurodivergent and/or autistic person) about sensory issues who did not have strong opinions on their individual sensory needs.

When designing spaces, events, and experiences for anyone, I suggest using inclusive design, which solves for one and serves many. Create sensory-friendly environments that would help accommodate the access and support needs of someone with sensory processing issues and you will create a sensory-friendly environment that will benefit everyone in the workplace.

Sensory-friendly environments significantly improve comfort, engagement, and productivity, as well as promote inclusion and belonging for all.

Consider that some people are hypersensitive and some people are hyposensitive. Spaces need to accommodate both.

Consider these accommodations for sensory friendly spaces:

- Lighting options: Provided adjustable lighting, allow for personal desk lamps, remove fluorescent and strobe lighting. Provide areas that are cozy and dark and areas with large windows to allow light and sunshine to come in.
- Noise management: Offer quiet spaces and noise canceling headphones, silent working areas, and areas that offer a variety of music choices and volumes. Recognize that the sound of a fan, AC/heat system, or any

appliances can be distracting or disabling to some.
- Flexible seating: Allow for standing desks, ball chairs, spinning chairs, soft chairs, chairs for one or couches for many as well as comfortable floor space options for seating.
- Scent-free policies: Implement fragrance-free policies to include strong smelling perfume, cologne, deodorant, essential oils, or hair products. Recognize the impact of strong scents as a distraction or impediment from someone from doing work such as cigarette/cigar smoke, chemicals, or mold.
- Visual stimulation: Some people prefer a clean, organized, uncluttered work environment whereas others prefer a more colorful and creative workspace. Offer quiet rooms with limited visual distractions and bright and active spaces.

Inclusive Design Practices are Proactive

Do not wait for someone to disclose a diagnosis or disability, or even an access or support need. Assume there are needs in the room. Interestingly, many people do not recognize their needs and disabilities until accommodations (such as sensory-friendly rooms or noise-canceling headphones) improve their ability to focus and feel safe at work.

Proactively solve for one and you serve many. Win-win.

Individual Coaching

Individual and group coaching can be particularly beneficial for neurodivergent employees as well as the people who lead them. Consider hiring a coach (like me!) to offer customized support around issues such as:

- Communication skills
- Executive functioning
- Time management

- Organization
- Emotional regulation
- Career coaching
- ADHD specific coaching

Clarity, Accuracy, and Transparency Matter

If you only want to attract autistic people, call it an autistic hiring program, not a neurodiversity hiring program. Neurodiversity is not synonymous with neurodivergent and neurodivergent is not synonymous with autism. This conversation is far more expansive, nuanced, and interesting.

A non-autistic neurodivergent person who applies to a neurodiversity- hiring program that is actually a misguided autistic hiring program ends up experiencing trauma and rejection as they are excluded from the very places that suggest they will finally be included. It's trauma on trauma and does a great bit of harm.

This level of disservice and harm reminds me of people and places that claim to be a "safe space". Please don't say that. One can never guarantee safety. Furthermore, someone who does not feel safe due to trauma or lived experiences of rejection, for example, feels worse when feeling unsafe in a supposed "safe space."

Rather, say "this is an intended safe space" or "this is a brave space." Clarity, accuracy, and transparency matter.

Another area of harm in neurodiversity hiring programs is when organizations specifically hire autistic people because research shows them to be 180% more productive, more able to hyper focus, and more willing to work overtime.

Not only are these stats based on stereotypes, but these hiring practices often lead to exploitation of autistic people and their unique strengths.

If you hire autistic people, or any neurodivergent people, please provide support systems and center accessibility in your policies and strategies.

12

Functioning Labels

The following is a brief, impactful, and immediately actionable call to action.

There are no "high-functioning" or "low functioning" people. Those are value judgments.

High or low according to who and what standards and expectations? That's right, neurotypical ones based on capitalism and patriarchy that do not account for different functioning styles.

Rather than use functioning labels for people, let us use these labels for society. Society is failing to function effectively, not the other way around.

For example, we have a "low-functioning" society that does not accommodate well for neurodivergent or disabled people well-yet.

When we talk to and about people, it is more respectful and inclusive to talk about access and support needs, not functioning levels. A person may have "high" or "low" support needs, but that does not mean anything about themselves as a human.

Shifting this language can help create cultures of inclusion, dignity, and civility.

13

Apparent and Non-Apparent Disabilities

When we discuss disability inclusion, it is important to understand the full spectrum of disabilities, including those that are immediately apparent and those that are not apparent at first. It is my current understanding after many discussions with people in the disability community that apparent and non- apparent disabilities is the preferred language, rather than "invisible" or "hidden" disabilities.

There are many reasons why the latter terms are offensive and dismissive to some, but I also want to reiterate that there are varied opinions on these terms. Just as with neurodivergence, the language is nuanced.

When in doubt... you guessed it, ATP. Ask the Person how they wish to identify and what language feels the most comfortable, accurate, and affirming to them.

80% of Disability is Non-Apparent

Research shows that 80% of disabilities are non-apparent. This includes neurodivergences, which includes mental health challenges, epilepsy, brain injury, and more. Current statistics show that 16% of the world is disabled. I have to assume these stats mostly reflect apparent disabilities, because if it is true that half of Gen Z and one third of millennials identify as disabled, and these generations make up 40% of our population, the numbers already don't add up.

Current research states that 20% of people struggle with mental illness (I am not a fan of that term and use mental health challenges) and, conservatively, 20% of people identify as neurodivergent. As mental health challenges and neurodivergence are often considered disabilities, the number of people who are disabled is certainly more than 16%.

That is the extent of my math tolerance. Numbers disable me—always have, thanks to dyscalculia.

Examples of Apparent and Non-Apparent Disabilities

Apparent disabilities include:

- Mobility issues requiring the use of a wheelchair or crutches
- Visual issues, including blindness
- Hearing issues, including deafness
- Some forms of cerebral palsy
- Certain types of limb differences or amputations

Non-apparent disabilities include:

- Chronic pain and arthritis
- Mental health challenges such as depression, anxiety, or PTSD
- Neurodevelopmental differences like autism or ADHD/VAST
- Learning disabilities such as dyslexia or dyscalculia
- Chronic illnesses like fibromyalgia, multiple sclerosis, or diabetes
- Sensory processing challenges

Notice I did not use words like "impairment" or "abnormality" or "special" to describe any of the disabilities. While there is no universal agreement on the use of these terms, it is best to use less subjective or judgmental terms such as "condition," or even less pathologizing, "experience," "issue," or "difference."

Use the term "accessible" over "handicapped" when referring to people or environments. "Handicapped" is outdated and focuses on what people cannot do, while "accessible" emphasizes the need for inclusion and access and focuses on what people can do. For example, rather than "handicapped bathroom," say "accessible bathroom."

We will all be disabled at one point or another, so accessibility should be prioritized by all. Disability can be permanent (as in vision challenges), temporary (as in a broken leg), or situational (as in someone who cannot hear or concentrate in a noisy environment). Given those nuances, think of all the times you have experienced disability and consider what access needs you had.

Have you benefited from a curb cut, elevator, headphones, or glasses before? I am guessing yes. Those tools allowed you to access an environment.

Accessibility simply means that people with disabilities have the same opportunities as people without disabilities. We have a long way to go before the workplace and society is fully accessible, but shifting language, mindsets, and awareness prepare us to do so.

Disabled by Society

Many disabled people say they are "disabled by society," meaning that disability is something that happens when people face barriers in society. It is often society, not one's innateness, that disables people. Disability happens when the world we live in is, for the most part, designed with the assumption that everyone has the same abilities.

Masking

The process by which neurodivergent or non-apparently disabled individuals hide or suppress their innate traits to stay safe or fit in with neurotypical expectations. While masking is physically and emotionally exhausting, it should be noted that masking is not "wrong" and does often keep people safe or open to opportunities such as jobs. There is also an intersectional component here.

For example, an unmasked Black, trans, neurodivergent person is far more disadvantaged and in danger of being unemployed than an unmasked white, cisgender, neurodivergent person, who could very likely be the CEO of a Fortune 100 company. Intersectionality has to be centered in discussions about the neurodivergent experience.

14

Social vs. Medical Model of Disability

Understanding the difference between the social and medical models of disability is crucial as we shift the responsibility to adapt away from the person and towards society.

The medical model is a traditional view that focuses on the individual's "problem" to be "fixed," "treated," or "cured." It places the onus on the disabled person to adapt to their environment.

The social model is a more progressive approach, recognizing that society creates barriers that disable people.It emphasizes that it is society's responsibility to remove these barriers and create inclusive environments and equitable opportunities for everyone to thrive.

The social model shifts our focus from "fixing" individuals to fixing our societal structures, attitudes, and environments. It's not the person who is disabled, but rather the society that is disabling.

Disabled people often face significant physical accessibility challenges in society as well as emotional accessibility challenges, including:

- Stigma: Misconceptions and negative attitudes about disabilities lead to

social isolation and reduced opportunities.
- Biases: Unconscious biases affect hiring decisions, social interactions, and overall treatment.
- Bullying and Harassment: Higher risk of experiencing bullying or harassment in educational and workplace settings.

Psychological Safety

Many individuals with non-apparent disabilities may choose not to disclose their disability in fear of stigma and discrimination. It is paramount that organizations work on establishing cultures of psychological safety, where sharing identities as well as access and support needs is encouraged and accommodations are honored.

I believe that only when those most vulnerable, those with the most intersecting marginalized and underrepresented identities, feel safe sharing ideas, offering feedback,and showing up to work as their authentic selves (without fear of negative consequences), does an organization have a chance at being a psychologically safe place to work.

Disclosure and Diagnosis Intersects with Privilege

The ability to receive a diagnosis or choose to disclose a disability often intersects with various forms of privilege. Factors such as socioeconomic status, race, gender, and access to healthcare can significantly impact an individual's ability to receive a formal diagnosis or feel safe disclosing their disability.

Consider how complicated, expensive, time and resource consuming it is to find a medical or mental health provider for the most privileged of people. Now consider how challenging it must be for people who cannot afford a diagnostic test or independently access transportation to appointments.

Imagine the challenge of accessing medical care if you are non-verbal or accessing mental healthcare in an English-speaking agency if you do not speak English. There are numerous examples of how privilege intersects with diagnosis and care management.

Disclosure intersects with privilege because of stigma, bias, discrimination, and lack of awareness. The experience of a white, cisgender, straight autistic man disclosing disability in the workplace is far, FAR different from, for example, a disabled, Black, trans, autistic man in the workplace. The former likely has a leadership role and may even be in the C-suite (check out the leaders of Fortune 100 companies). The latter is lucky if they even make it past the interview process.

Not so fun fact: 80% of college educated autistic people are unemployed. The reason? NOT incompetence or an unwillingness to work. The reason in that case is likely a combination of bias, ableism, and transphobia. In our current culture, white, cisgender people, specifically wealthy men, have more power, privilege, and opportunities than others. More on all that in my next book—standby.

Our goal is to create cultures of neuroinclusion where all minds and bodies can thrive. Also don't forget the benefits of a diverse workforce-increased innovation, problem-solving, collaboration, retention, loyalty, and so on.

Neuroinclusion and disability inclusion is good for the bottom line and good for humanity. Win, win.

15

Superpower or Disability? Yes, And.

When discussing neurodivergence and disability, we often encounter two seemingly opposing narratives: the idea of these differences as "superpowers" versus the traditional view of them as disabilities or challenges. And while the superpower narrative is a positive stereotype, it is still an over-generalization that does not honor lived experience. The reality is far more nuanced.

In this chapter, we'll explore a more balanced perspective that acknowledges both the unique strengths and the real challenges that come with neurodivergence and disability.

Many disabled people do not appreciate the phrase "superpower" because it disregards the real challenges of disability and can perpetuate the idea that saying disability is wrong. Being strength-based is neuroinclusive, telling someone they aren't disabled, they have superpowers is dismissive and offensive.

Telling someone they have superpowers also puts unnecessary pressure on them to perform well and never show weakness. This could easily lead to hesitancy to ask for help or share access needs, which will undoubtedly lead to burnout.

There is also a paradox many neurodivergent people experience. Yes, they may have "superpowers" such as increased awareness, intuition, and sensitivities. But those very abilities are disabling when they become overstimulating or overwhelming.

An anxious person can have superpowers of sensing and, thus, preventing danger, and at the same time, be disabled by the anxiety of hyper awareness and a constant planning for worst case scenarios.

An ADHDer can have the superpower of hyper focusing and finish writing a book in a day while at the same time, be disabled by their inability to remember to eat or pick up their kids from school during this period of hyper focusing.

As always, it is most important to ATP how they identify, what language they prefer to use, and what their access and support needs are.

Spiky Profiles

A helpful way to understand the neurodivergent experience is through the concept of "spiky profiles." This term refers to the uneven distribution of abilities and challenges that many neurodivergent individuals experience.

Imagine a graph where different skills and abilities are represented. For a neurotypical person, this graph might show a relatively even distribution across various areas. For a neurodivergent individual, however, the graph might show dramatic peaks in some areas(representing exceptional abilities) and valleys in others (representing significant challenges).

For example, an autistic individual might have exceptional pattern recognition skills and attention to detail, but struggle with social communication. Someone with ADHD/VAST might be highly creative and able to hyper-focus on tasks they're passionate about but have difficulty with sustained attention on less engaging tasks. Often "easy" things are hard, and "hard" things are easy. It's a paradox!

Understanding spiky profiles helps us move beyond the simplistic "superpower vs. disability" dichotomy. It acknowledges that neurodivergent individuals often have both significant strengths and challenges, which can vary greatly from person to person.

Agency and Autonomy

Just as with language preferences, it is important to respect each individual's agency in how they view and describe their own neurodivergence or disability. Some may embrace the "superpower" narrative, finding it empowering and validating of their strengths. Others may prefer to focus on the challenges they face and the support they need.

Often, there is the assumption that neurodivergent and disabled people are incompetent, need extra help, or have "special needs." These assumptions can lead to patronizing and infantilizing statements, disguised as care.

Rather than "let me help you" or "how can I help you," consider " here if you need help." The key is to avoid imposing any single narrative on all neurodivergent or disabled individuals.

Instead, we should create space for each person to define their own experience and needs and, you guessed it - ATP (Ask The Person)!

Media Stereotypes and Stigma

Media portrayals of neurodivergence and disability often fall into problematic stereotypes:

- The Savant: Portraying all autistic individuals as having extraordinary abilities, such as in math or memory. You have met one autistic person,

you have met one autistic person. Do not use or assume "genius" or the term "Rain Man," unless they identify as such.
- The Inspirational Story: Framing disability as something to "overcome" or "endure" rather than a part of human diversity. Saying you are "inspiring" or "brave" to a disabled person implies that they are continuing to take action, despite having a terrible circumstance.
- The Burden: Depicting disabled individuals as overwhelming to and dependent on others. You would be surprised at how often people say "you are a lot."

One interesting and also potentially harmful piece of research from JP Morgan found that autistic people are 140% more productive than their neurotypical peers. This would explain why there are so many "neurodiversity hiring programs" that are actually autistic hiring programs. My concern is that autistic people will be taken advantage of and overworked.

When an autistic person is passionate about work, they may very well be 140% more productive than their neurotypical coworkers. They may hyperfocus and not realize how hard they are working until they reach the stage of overwhelm, burnout, and exhaustion. The exploitation of autistic people by organizations that hire them, hoping they will work beyond their scheduled and paid hours, is a major concern.

It is important to note that the unemployment rate for autistic people is as high as 85% in the U.S. I believe this is due to stigma and bias in the interview process, inaccessible workplaces, and a need for autistic people to "mask" as neurotypical to feel safe and keep their jobs.

These numbers also reflect autistic people who were hired through neurodiversity programs that may have had neurodiversity-affirming policies but lacked strategies or systems of accountability to back them up.

Neither ableism nor stereotypes, including toxically positive ones like "superpowers," have a place in work environments. Let's respect the full range of individualized experiences.

Masking

When any neurodivergent person masks or feels the need to hide or disguise parts of themselves to remain safe or accepted in the workplace, it takes a toll. Masking is physically and mentally exhausting and often leads to serious health consequences such as depression, anxiety, chronic pain, and burnout—all of which often lead to needing time off or not being able to work at all.

While I would love to suggest all neurodivergent people unapologetically unmask and share their authentic selves, I recognize it is not always safe to do so. Intersecting marginalized identities play a part in the decision process and these dynamics must be honored. Allow people to reveal their identities at their own time and pace.

Some people may not even know they are neurodivergent or recognize that they have been masking most of their lives. The practice of neuronormativity is ingrained in our lives from childhood, similar to how hetero and cisnormative standards are.

There is usually a catalyst movement that leads people to realize they are not neurotypical and that most of their lives they have been masking to "keep up" or "play the game." Common catalyst moments include children receiving diagnosis and requiring accommodations at school, menopause (yes, hormones change our brains and functioning abilities), and burnout.

The majority of my clients realized they were neurodivergent during the Covid pandemic, when they were asked to participate in remote learning or remote work for the first time, which highlighted individualized access and support needs in ways that were never more clear.

16

Accessibility Best Practices

Accessibility warrants its own book and the importance of accessibility in any inclusive culture cannot be overstated. What good is any of this if our work spaces and experiences are not accessible? We are not only accommodating those with apparent and non-apparent disabilities, but we are also creating inclusive spaces for all minds and bodies to have equitable opportunity to thrive at work.

All employers have the responsibility to provide employees with a safe, inclusive, and accessible workplace as defined by the legislative frameworks in their country. Compliance with these frameworks (such as ADA in America) is mandatory and helps businesses avoid fines and lawsuits. Steps employers take to create a more accessible workplace include:

- Physical accessibility is providing accessible facilities such as parking spaces and bathrooms, ramps, automatic doors, lower desks, enough space for wheelchairs and other assisted devices to fit and function. Use "accessible parking" and "accessible bathrooms," rather than handi-capped.
- Digital accessibility is providing transcripts, closed captions, alt text, accessible fonts and colors, and assistive technologies. Make slide decks accessible.

- Information accessibility is providing clear communication in a variety of modalities. Some people prefer receiving information through emails, others through videos or in-person conversations. Some visual learners benefit from charts and graphs over words or numbers.

Accessibility ensures that everyone can fully participate in and contribute to the organization, regardless of their physical or neurological differences and regardless of whether there are apparent or non-apparent disabilities. Go beyond physical accommodations to include considerations for cognitive accessibility, sensory needs, and flexible work arrangements.

Performative vs Non-Performative Measures

It's important to distinguish between performative and non-performative accessibility measures. Performative measures are superficial actions taken primarily for show, without creating meaningful change. Non- performative measures, on the other hand, involve substantial, systemic changes that genuinely improve accessibility.

Here are some key principles for implementing non-performative accessibility measures:

- Proactive Implementation: Don't wait for someone to request accommodations. Build accessibility into all aspects of your organization from the ground up.
- Continuous Improvement: Treat accessibility as an ongoing process, not a one-time fix. Regularly assess and update your practices.
- Inclusive Design: Implement solutions that benefit everyone but are specifically designed for accessibility. Solve for one, serve many.
- Meaningful Consultation: Involve neurodivergent and disabled individuals in the development and implementation of accessibility measures.
- Measurable Outcomes: Set concrete goals for accessibility and track your progress.

- Hold people accountable to follow the accessibility policies and strategies.

When crafting your organization's accessibility policy, consider including:

- A clear statement of commitment to accessibility
- Specific accessibility standards you adhere to
- How accessibility is considered in your products, services, and workplace
- Training and awareness programs for staff
- Procurement policies that prioritize accessible products and services
- How you engage with the disability community
- A process for reporting accessibility issues and requesting accommodations
- Regular audits and updates to your accessibility measures

An effective accessibility policy is not just about compliance with legal requirements. It is about creating a culture where accessibility is valued and prioritized at all levels of the organization.

Ableism

Ableism is discrimination, prejudice, or bias against disabled people. It manifests in attitudes, behaviors, policies, and social structures that devalue, stereotype, or exclude individuals based on their physical, mental, or sensory abilities. Ableism can be both overt, such as physical barriers that prevent wheelchair access, and subtle (but equally harmful), such as assumptions that people with disabilities are inherently less capable or need "fixing."

Examples of ableism include:

- Environmental Barriers: Lack of accessible materials, buildings, transportation, bathrooms, and technology. Lack of sensory friendly spaces and experiences.
- Stereotyping and Stigmatizing: Labeling people with disabilities as

"inspirational" simply for managing their daily lives or assuming they need pity or assistance when they may not. Re-framing disability as "superpowers" without asking the disabled person.
- Policy and Structural Discrimination: Exclusionary practices in employment, healthcare, and education. Accommodations are not "special treatment" or privileges, they are human rights that give people equitable opportunity to thrive.

The disability justice movement seeks to combat ableism by promoting accessibility, inclusive design, and societal changes that value disability as a natural part of the human experience, advocating for equality and recognition of disability rights as human rights.

17

Neuroinclusive Policies

Creating neuroinclusive policies begins with asking the right questions. By framing our inquiries in an inclusive manner, we can develop policies that truly address the needs of all individuals, neurodivergent and neurotypical alike. In this chapter, we'll explore a series of questions that can guide us towards more neuroinclusive policy development.

The Power of Inclusive Questions

Inclusive questions help us challenge our assumptions, uncover hidden biases, and consider perspectives we might otherwise overlook. They push us to think beyond the neurotypical experience and consider the diverse and unique support and access needs of all employees.

Sample Questions for Neuroinclusive Policy Development

Recruitment and Hiring:

- How can we make our job descriptions more accessible and appealing to neurodivergent candidates?
- Are our interview processes accommodating different communication styles and sensory needs?

- How can we assess skills and potential without relying solely on traditional interview formats?

Workplace Environment:

- How can we create sensory-friendly spaces within our office?
- What flexible work arrangements can we offer to accommodate different needs and working styles?
- How can we make our meetings more inclusive for those who process information differently?

Performance Management:

- Are our performance metrics flexible enough to recognize different working styles and strengths?
- How can we provide feedback in ways that are clear and constructive for neurodivergent employees?
- Are we considering neurodivergent traits as potential strengths rather than limitations?

Professional Development:

- How can we make our training programs more accessible to different learning styles?
- Are we offering mentorship opportunities that support neurodivergent employees?
- How can we create career paths that value and utilize neurodivergent strengths?

Company Culture:

- How can we educate all employees about neurodiversity and create a culture of acceptance?

- Are our social events and team-building activities inclusive of different sensory and social needs?
- How can we encourage and value diverse thinking styles in problem-solving and innovation?

Communication:

- Are our communication channels accessible to those who may struggle with certain forms of interaction?
- How can we make our written communications clearer and more direct?
- Are we providing multiple ways for employees to share ideas and concerns?

Accommodations:

- How can we proactively offer accommodations without requiring disclosure of diagnoses?
- Are our accommodation processes clear, simple, and non-stigmatizing?
- How can we create a culture where requesting accommodations is normalized and encouraged?

Leadership and Advancement:

- How can we identify and nurture leadership potential in neurodivergent employees?
- Are our promotion criteria inclusive of different working and communication styles?
- How can we ensure neurodivergent perspectives are represented in decision-making processes?

Neuroinclusive Questions in Action

When developing or reviewing policies, use these questions as a starting point. Engage with neurodivergent employees or consultants to refine and expand on these questions based on lived experiences.

The goal is not just to have the right answers, but to consistently ask the right questions. This approach ensures that neuroinclusion is an ongoing consideration in all aspects of your organization's policies and practices.

For example, ask "what is your preferred method of communication?" and then honor it. Some people prefer in-person conversations while others prefer email, phone calls, or text.

By centering these inclusive questions in your policy development process, you are taking the foundational step towards creating a truly neuroinclusive culture. You are moving beyond surface-level accommodations to deeply consider how every aspect of your organization can be more welcoming and supportive of neurodivergent and neurotypical individuals alike.

18

Inclusive Design

In creating truly neuroinclusive environments, we need to shift our approach from reactive accommodation to proactive accessibility and support. This is where the principles of inclusive design come into play. These concepts not only benefit neurodivergent and disabled individuals but can enhance the experience for everyone in your organization.

The "Solve for One, Serve Many" Principle

At the heart of inclusive design is the "Solve for One, Serve Many" principle. This approach suggests that by designing solutions for individuals with specific access and support needs, we often create innovations and systems that benefit a much wider group.

Microsoft, the leader in inclusive design, offers some compelling examples:

- Closed captions, originally designed for deaf users, now benefit anyone watching video in a noisy environment or learning a new language.
- Voice-to-text technology, developed for individuals with mobility impairments, is now widely used for convenience by many people.
- High-contrast modes, crucial for some visually impaired users, can reduce eye strain for anyone working long hours on screens.

The classic example is curb cuts, the cut-out ramps on sidewalks designed for wheelchair users, but appreciated and enjoyed by bicyclists and those using strollers, walkers, and shopping carts. Solve for one, serve many.

Proactive Accessibility Planning-Assume Access Needs

To implement inclusive design effectively, we need to move beyond waiting for accommodation requests. Instead, we should assume diverse access and support needs from the outset. Here's how to approach proactive accessibility planning:

- Build Flexibility into Systems: Create systems that can easily adapt to individual needs without requiring extensive modifications.
- Consider Digital Accessibility: Ensure that all digital tools and platforms used in your organization are accessible. This includes websites, internal communication tools, and any software used for daily tasks.
- Anticipate Access and Support Needs: When designing any process, policy, or space, consider a wide range of potential needs. Think about sensory sensitivities, different communication styles, varied cognitive processing, and physical accessibility.
- Involve Diverse Perspectives: Include neurodivergent and disabled people in your design and planning processes. Their lived experiences are invaluable in identifying potential barriers and innovative solutions.
- Create Sensory-Friendly Spaces: Design physical environments with consideration for sensory sensitivities. This might include quiet zones, adjustable lighting, and options for standing or alternative seating.
- Offer Information in Multiple Formats: Provide important information in various formats (written, verbal, visual) to cater to different processing styles.
- Implement Clear Wayfinding: Use clear, consistent signage and intuitive layouts to make navigation easier for everyone.
- Regular Accessibility Audits: Conduct regular audits of your physical and digital environments to identify and address any accessibility issues.

Beyond Accessible Technology

While accessible technology is critical, it's important to remember that access extends beyond digital tools. Consider:

- Flexible Work Arrangements: Offer options for remote work, flexible hours, or alternative work setups.
- Diverse Meeting Formats: Provide agendas in advance, allow for written contributions, and consider alternatives to traditional meeting structures.
- Clear Communication Protocols: Establish clear guidelines for communication that accommodate different styles and needs.
- Inclusive Social Events: Ensure that team-building and social activities are designed with diverse needs in mind.

By embracing inclusive design, we create environments that are not just accommodating of differences but are fundamentally designed to welcome and support diversity.

This approach leads to more innovative, adaptable, engaged, and ultimately more successful teams and organizations.

The goal is not to create a one-size-fits-all solution, but rather a flexible, adaptable, and accessible environment. By solving for one, we truly can serve many.

19

Access and Support Needs

As we continue to cultivate cultures of neuroinclusion, we value continued efforts towards inclusive language, proactive accessibility, and peopling. A focus on privacy and agency takes center stage. We shift from asking for specific diagnoses in order to create accommodations to asking about access and support needs.

This approach not only respects privacy but also creates a more flexible and responsive system that can benefit all employees, regardless of whether they identify as neurodivergent or disabled.

Focus on Needs, Not Labels

What if a formal diagnosis was not necessary for accommodations? Rather than categorizing individuals based on diagnoses or neurotypes, consider framing policies and accommodations around specific access and support needs. For example:

- Rather than "accommodations for ADHD/VAST," think about "support for focus and time management."
- Instead of "autism-friendly spaces," consider "sensory-friendly environments."

- Replace "dyslexia accommodations" with "reading and writing support options."

This needs-based approach has several advantages:

- Inclusivity: Benefiting anyone who might have similar needs, regardless of diagnosis.
- Flexibility: Allowing for personalized support that can adapt as needs change.
- Destigmatization: Normalizing the idea that everyone has different needs and styles.
- Privacy: Not requiring individuals to disclose specific diagnoses to receive support.

Not everyone has a formal diagnosis and not everyone can access or afford a formal diagnosis. Diagnosis and disclosure intersect with privilege (details below). Some may choose not to disclose for personal or professional reasons. The needs-based approach respects privacy, agency, and autonomy.

Diagnosis and Disclosure Intersects with Privilege

It's important to recognize that the ability to receive a diagnosis or choose to disclose often intersects with various forms of privilege:

- Economic Privilege: Diagnostic processes can be expensive and time-consuming, making them inaccessible to many.
- Cultural Factors: Some cultures may have different perspectives on neurodiversity and disability, affecting an individual's likelihood of seeking diagnosis or disclosing.
- Gender and Racial Biases: Historical biases in diagnostic criteria and healthcare can make it harder for certain groups to receive accurate diagnoses.
- Educational Access: Those with higher levels of education may be more

likely to recognize neurodivergent traits in themselves and seek diagnosis.
- Employment Status: Fear of job loss or discrimination may prevent some from seeking diagnosis or disclosing in the workplace.

Steps towards a needs-based approach:

- Review current policies: Identify where you might be requiring unnecessary disclosure or specific diagnoses for support.
- Train managers: Educate leadership on how to have conversations about needs without requiring disclosure of personal medical information.
- Offer universal supports: Implement supports that anyone can access without needing to identify as neurodivergent or disabled.
- Create a needs assessment: Develop a voluntary, confidential way for employees to communicate their access and support needs without having to disclose.
- Foster open communication: Create a culture where discussing work needs and preferences is normalized for all employees.

By focusing on access and support needs rather than formal diagnoses, we can create safer and more equitable systems for all.

20

Barriers to Neuroinclusion

Cultivating a neuroinclusive culture requires a proactive approach to identifying and removing barriers that may prevent full participation, engagement, and belonging for neurodivergent and disabled individuals. These barriers can be physical, attitudinal, informational, or communicational. Let's systematically address common barriers and how to remove them.

Common Barriers to Neuroinclusion

Ableist and Inaccessible Barriers: These are often rooted in assumptions about "normal" abilities and can unintentionally exclude neurodivergent and disabled individuals. Examples include:

- Inflexible work schedules
- Overstimulating work environments
- Rigid communication expectations

Physical Barriers: While often associated with mobility challenges, physical barriers can also affect neurodivergent individuals. Consider:

- Lack of quiet spaces for focus or sensory breaks

- Inadequate lighting options
- Absence of adjustable workstations

Attitudinal Barriers: These are often the most challenging to overcome as they involve changing mindsets and organizational culture. Examples include:

- Stereotypes about neurodivergent individuals' capabilities
- Lack of understanding about non-apparent disabilities, including mental health
- Resistance to providing accommodations and seeing them as "privileges."

Informational/Communication Barriers: These barriers prevent effective exchange of information. They might include:

- Over-reliance on a single communication method (e.g., only verbal instructions)
- Lack of clear, concise written documentation
- Absence of visual aids or alternative formats for important information

Strategies for Removing Barriers to Neuroinclusion

Conduct Regular Accessibility Audits:

- Regularly assess your physical and digital environments for potential barriers
- Involve neurodivergent and disabled employees in these audits

Implement Inclusive Design Principles:

- Design spaces and processes that are usable by the widest range of people possible, but specifically designed to meet access and support needs
- Provide multiple means of engagement, representation, and expression

Offer Flexible Work Arrangements:

- Allow for remote work options
- Provide flexible start and end times
- Offer alternative meeting formats (e.g., walking meetings, written discussions)

Create Sensory-Friendly Environments:

- Provide quiet spaces or zones
- Offer noise-canceling headphones
- Install adjustable or varied lighting

Improve Communication Practices:

- Provide information in multiple formats (written, verbal, visual)
- Use clear, concise language in all communications
- Offer advance notice for meetings and changes

Provide Ongoing Education and Training

- Offer neurodiversity and disability awareness training for all employees
- Educate managers on inclusive leadership practices

Establish Clear Accommodation Processes:

- Create simple, transparent processes for requesting accommodations
Ensure that accommodations are provided in a timely manner

Foster an Inclusive Culture:

- Celebrate neurodiversity and disability as valuable aspects of diversity
- Encourage open dialogues about different working styles and needs

Review and Update Policies:

- Ensure that all policies are inclusive and do not unintentionally discriminate
- Include neurodivergent and disabled employees in policy development

Leverage Technology:

- Utilize assistive technologies and ensure all digital platforms are accessible
- Provide training on available accessibility features in commonly used software

Removing barriers is an ongoing process. What works for one person may not work for another, and needs can change over time. The key is to remain flexible, open to feedback, and committed to continuous improvement.

21

Strengths-Based Approach

One of the most transformative shifts we can make is moving from a deficit-based model to a strengths-based approach. This change in perspective, dramatically improves how we think about and talk about ourselves and others.

Focus on Strengths, Not Deficits

Traditionally, neurodivergence has been viewed through a lens of deficits or challenges. However, a strengths-based approach recognizes and leverages the unique abilities that often accompany neurodivergent traits.

Examples of neurodivergent strengths:

- Autistic individuals may excel at pattern recognition and attention to detail.
- People with ADHD/VAST often demonstrate high creativity and the ability to hyper-focus.
- Dyslexic individuals frequently show strong spatial reasoning and big-picture thinking.
- Chronically ill individuals show strong resilience and adaptability.
- Anxious people are cautious and can often sense danger and conflict before

others.

By focusing on these strengths, we not only empower neurodivergent individuals but also enhance our organizations' capabilities.

To implement a strength-based approach:

- Identify and celebrate individual strengths during performance reviews and daily recognitions. Some prefer private recognition, while others prefer public recognition.
- Create opportunities that allow employees to leverage their unique abilities. Match strengths and skills with tasks and projects.
- Encourage diverse problem-solving approaches that capitalize on different thinking/learning/functioning styles. Stay open to new and non-linear ways to solve problems.

Note that a strength-based approach does not mean re-framing or dismissing a person's lived experience. For example, it is not strength-based to tell someone who identifies with disability that they simply have "superpowers."

Create space for people to claim their own identity, strengths, access, support needs, and unique ways of functioning... and then believe them.

That's Peopling 101.

22

Accountability

I am going to make this chapter short in hopes everyone will read it in its entirety and then take action to implement the strategies for accountability. Having neuroinclusive policies is NOTHING without strategy and accountability. In order to cultivate and continue to nurture cultures of neuroinclusion, you must hold yourself, your organization, and anyone who violates policies accountable.

Anti-bullying/Harassment Policies and Strategies

Ensure that your anti-bullying and harassment policies explicitly protect neurodivergent and disabled individuals.

These policies should:

- Clearly define what constitutes discrimination or harassment.
- Provide examples of unacceptable behavior and language.
- Outline the process for reporting and addressing incidents.
- Emphasize that microaggressions are forms of discrimination.
- Provide ongoing training on stigma, bias, microaggressions, and bullying (i.e. Call me).
- Hold people accountable and implement consequences for bullying and/or

harassment.

Leaders, make sure your own actions and strategies stay aligned with your policies. Lead by example. Stay humble, curious, and empathetic. Treat all minds and bodies with respect. Listen to and honor lived experience. Offer accommodations for access and support needs. Model the ongoing efforts of cultivating cultures of neuroinclusion.

23

Intersectionality

Neurodivergence and disability do not exist in isolation; they intersect with all other aspects of identity, such as race, gender, sexuality, and age. I believe intersectionality is at the heart of any impactful framework for inclusivity and peopling.

Intersectionality (or intersectional theory)is a term first coined in 1989 by American civil rights advocate and leading scholar of critical race theory, Kimberle Williams Crenshaw. The theory examines how various biological, social, and cultural categories of identity interact on multiple and simultaneous levels.

When thinking about intersectionality in disability, most disabled people will face systemic inequalities such as lack of accommodations, but a disabled person can also face added barriers such as unemployment, discrimination, cultural stigmas, barriers to accessing healthcare, or limited educational opportunities due to their race, gender, religion, or socioeconomic identity.

When neurodiversity and disability intersect with various other identities, it magnifies the complexity and experiences of systemic oppression. Consider cultural and language barriers, socioeconomic barriers, and race barriers as they intersect with work, accessibility, and healthcare. Remember diagnosis and disclosure intersect with privilege.

To honor intersectionality in the workplace:

- Recognize multiple identities: Understand that individuals may face compound challenges or bring multifaceted perspectives based on their intersecting identities.
- Avoid generalizations: Remember that neurodivergent and disabled experiences can vary widely based on other aspects of identity and individual circumstances.
- Create inclusive support systems: Ensure that employee resource groups (ERGs) and support networks are welcoming and accessible to individuals with multiple marginalized identities.
- Consider intersectional ERGs: Employee resource groups that recognize intersecting identities, such as neurodivergence and BIPOC, bring an even greater sense of belonging and inclusion.

Example of Intersectional Impact - the Black ADHD Experience

Exploring the intersections of the Black and ADHD experience highlight continued stigma and injustice, starting in elementary schools and continuing into adulthood. It should be noted that ADHD diagnosis is still made in geographical, cultural, and racial context.

Here are some interesting, but discouraging U.S. facts:

- Black children are 70% less likely to receive an official ADHD diagnosis than their white classmates.
- Historical oppression and mistreatment cause Black parents to be more reluctant to seek ADHD diagnosis or medical care for their children.
- Black children diagnosed with ADHD are more likely to be disciplinarily removed from their classrooms for being disruptive.
- The racial bias and over diagnosis of coexisting conditions such as ODD,

Oppositional Defiant Disorder, often result in more punitive consequences and removal from the classroom for Black children.
- White children, on the other hand, are more likely to receive a diagnosis of PDA, Pathological Demand Avoidance, which has been re-framed as Persistent Drive for Autonomy or simply Demand Avoidance, and are more likely to receive services than punishment.
- Black children are more likely to face criminal prosecution for problem behavior, resulting in the school-to-prison pipeline.
- One quarter (25%) of incarcerated adults have ADHD and at least half are neurodivergent.

"Black kids get cops, white kids get docs" should not be a common saying. And yet, it is, because it is often true. Black ADHD kids grow up to be Black ADHD adults.

The problem is complex. The solution is a multi-system and multi-level response, including:

- Unpacking stigma and bias about race, mental health, and differences.
- Paradigm shifts from the pathology paradigm to the neurodiversity paradigm.
- Improving access to services in schools and health care centers.
- Establishing and earning trust from the Black community.
- Holding individuals and organizations accountable for discrimination.

Organizations must be aware of the impact of intersectionality and how the multiple intersecting identities of people affect their physical, mental, emotional, and social well-being and ability to thrive at work.

24

Neurodiversity/LGBTQIA+ Affirming

If you say you are neurodiversity-affirming, you also must be LGBTQIA+ and gender affirming. The intersection between neurodivergence and LGBTQIA+ identities is strong and growing stronger by the day given how younger generations are diverging from and queering norms.

The goal is to affirm ALL of the ways people diverge from norms. Interestingly, when people learn and unlearn neurotypical performance and expectations, they are simultaneously learning and unlearning other norms, such as heteronormativity or cisnormativity.

When you question or queer one norm, you begin to question and queer all norms. This often results in a fierce unraveling of norms and a new expansiveness. It is not uncommon for people to "come out" neurodivergent and queer at around the same time. Affirming professionals hold space for this journey.

While we need far more research on the subject, it is true that a large percentage of neurodivergent people identify as LGBTQIA+, queer, or gender non-conforming. In the autistic community, for example, research shows up to 70% identify as LGBTQIA+.

This is NOT to say that all neurodivergent people identify as LGBTQIA+; however, I would argue that anyone who identifies as LGBTQIA+ is neurodivergent. Remember that neurodivergent is an identity used by anyone who diverges from neuronormativity, or society's current idea of what is "normal," "right," or "ideal."

Ways to be LGBTQIA+ and gender affirming at work include:

- Share your pronouns and honor other people's pronouns.
- Apologize and quickly correct yourself if you misgender someone.
- When in doubt, use "they" rather than "she" or "he."
- Provide gender-neutral bathrooms.
- Use gender-neutral language (such as "Y'all" or "everyone" vs "ladies and gentlemen").
- Stay educated and current on LGBTQIA+ issues.
- Actively listen to coworkers about their lived experiences.
- Support inclusive and anti-bullying policies.
- Speak up against microaggressions and harassment.
- Implement parental leave for all employees.
- Offer LGBTQIA+ and intersectional Employee Resource Groups (ERGs).
- Promote psychological safety, especially for those with marginalized identities.
- Provide insurance for mental health and gender affirming care.

Offer continued education and training on affirming practices. (call ME!)

As with any affirming practices, it is important to be an active ally, be open to learning and unlearning, and treat everyone with respect, regardless of their gender identity, sexual orientation, disability, or neuro functioning.

The future of work is neuroqueer! Are you ready?

25

Leading Neurodiverse Teams

Want enthusiastically engaged talent? Of course you do! To effectively engage and lead neurodiverse teams, and specifically neurodivergent talent, leaders can implement strategies that support different access, cognitive, sensory, and communication needs.

The following best practices were designed to accommodate the access and support needs of autistic and ADHD/VAST talent but notice that all of these practices benefit ALL people, neurodivergent and neurotypical alike. The essence of neuroinclusion and peopling is treating all people with respect and care.

Best Practices for Leading Neurodiverse Teams:

- Respect and affirm Lived Experience and Identities
- Respect, affirm, and believe the lived experiences and identities. Validate unique perspectives. Foster psychological safety and trust. Acknowledge the impact of intersectionality.
- ATP (Ask The Person) how they identify and what their access and support needs are.
- Accessible Materials, Meetings, and Spaces
- Ensure materials, presentations, and meeting formats are accessible.

For example, use clear language and visual supports, provide agendas beforehand, and record meetings for later review.
- Sensory-friendly environments—avoiding harsh lighting or excessive noise—help people stay focused and comfortable by limiting distractions and offering flexible choices for work spaces.
- Consider a basket in the middle of your conference table with a variety of quiet fidget toys, noise-canceling headphones, or blank paper for doodling (which often helps keep brains engaged).

Accommodate Diverse Learning, Thinking, and Communication Styles

- Respect different communication styles. Some may prefer written communication over verbal, and others may need additional time to process information before responding.
- Neurodivergent individuals may have distinct learning and processing styles. Support their engagement by offering options such as visual aids, written and verbal instructions, and flexible timelines. Recognize and celebrate these differences by focusing on strengths rather than deficits.
- Focus more on what is being expressed, rather than how it is being expressed.
- Recognize people in the way they prefer. Some people prefer private recognition, while others prefer public recognition.
- Use neuroinclusive questions to establish neuroinclusive policies and strategies.

Flexible Working Hours

- Many neurodivergent individuals thrive with flexibility in their work schedules. Allowing remote work, flexible hours, or personalized work spaces can lead to better performance and satisfaction.
- Not everyone's energy and concept of time aligns with the traditional 9-5 work structure. Some people experience their best ideas and energy in the early morning or evening. Especially if the work is project-based,

allow people flexibility to complete tasks in alignment with their unique rhythms.
- Allow people freedom to work with, rather than against, their innate desires and needs to hyper-focus or use urgency for fuel. Allow people the autonomy to rest as needed between energy bursts.

Create Psychologically Safe (Brave) Spaces

- Cultivate an environment where all employees feel comfortable sharing ideas and concerns without fear of repercussions. Recognize intersecting identities, as employees may experience compounded challenges and fears if they belong to multiple underrepresented groups.
- Take time and care to specifically include those with the most intersecting marginalized identities in feedback and decision processes.
- Don't claim "safe space" as we can never guarantee safety. We don't know what lived experiences and traumas people are coming into the workspace with. I suggest saying "this is an intended safe space" or "this is a brave space."

Listen to the Quiet People and Truth Tellers

- Often, it is the quiet or non-verbal people who hold all the answers to your culture problems. These are possible autistic people, highly-sensitive people, introverts, or non-verbal people who are highly aware and intuitive
- Autistic people in particular are known to be truth-tellers who notice systemic problems before anyone else is aware. They often refer to themselves as "canaries," in reference to canaries in the coal mines who determine if the air is safe. Autistic feedback is transparent and honest and often pointed. It is often misinterpreted as "too harsh" or "rude." Autistic people are often told they are not "team-players" when they offer feedback or criticism. An excellent book on this very subject is *The Canary Code*, by Ludmila N. Praslova, PhD.

Take Accountability for Continuous Improvement

- Foster open feedback channels to gain insights into the experiences of neurodivergent employees and adapt practices as needed. This approach signals to employees that their well- being and contributions matter.
- Offer regular professional development trainings on neuroinclusion, peopling, and accessibility (call ME!)
- Hold yourself and people accountable for biases, microaggressions, bullying, discrimination, and exclusion. Know better, do better.

Empower and Elevate Talent

- Leaders are not the only change agents. Empower people to be part of culture transformation and change, no matter their role.
- Notice who is at the decision table. Notice who is not invited.
- Give everyone the opportunity to contribute to the conversation.
- Foster open feedback channels so people know they are heard.
- Recognize people often and in the way they prefer to be recognized.
- Promote people so everyone has an equitable opportunity to thrive and rise.

26

Respect Rubric

Assessment tools and personality tests are designed to develop increased awareness of different learning and working styles. While tests like DISC, PI, MBTI, and Strengths Finder offer valuable insights into human behavior and aptitude, they were designed for normative populations.

The unique processing and functioning of many forms of neurodivergence can skew results and interpretations of the data. These assessment tools also require conversations between leaders and employees to explore the data and explain what the results mean for them at work, something many do not take the time to do.

Moving away from categorizing people through the language of universal tools and towards learning about unique strengths and preferences in the language of the employee offers more agency, inclusion, and useful information.

Many organizations request "user models"(sometimes called "personal operating manuals"), in order to understand team members' motivations, strengths, and communications styles. User models support leaders in creating effective management strategies that resonate with individuals' unique needs and goals, ultimately fostering higher engagement, productivity, and job satisfaction.

User models typically suggest topics for employees to write about, such as work style, communication style, and values. Open-ended questions are often difficult for people to answer, especially if someone is anxious or unsure of the context or parameters of a question. For example, one user model I came upon asked people to expand on the topic "what you do not have patience for."

Outside of the confusing wording, without context, a mind that diverges could go in many useful and not useful directions with that prompt. I imagined answers as brief and honest as "I do not have patience for user models" to extensive essays on capitalism, colonialism, and racism.

I propose a more neuroinclusive tool which I call the "Respect Rubric," which is based on neuroinclusive questions about specific preferences.

Similar to the user manual, the Respect Rubric creates an opportunity for increased awareness and clear dialogue around different learning, thinking, and communication styles.

It fosters psychological safety as the questions encourage agency, feedback, and authenticity. When shared with members of the team, there is increased empathy and an understanding of how to best accommodate each other's access, support, and sensory needs.

The Respect Rubric Includes 7 Key Neuroinclusive Topics and Questions

- **R**: RECOGNITION/FEEDBACK - How do you prefer to receive recognition and feedback? (i.e. publicly, privately, via email or in person)
- **E**: ENVIRONMENT - What type of work environment do you thrive in? (i.e. hybrid, remote, open area with sunlight or enclosed area with minimal light)
- **S**: SUPPORT - What are your access and support needs and how can we accommodate? (i.e. transcripts, standing desks, mental health days)
- **P**: PRODUCTIVITY - What are your favorite organizational and productivity tools?
- **E**: ENERGY - What helps you remain in flow and able to innovate and collaborate?
- **C**: COMMUNICATION - What are your communication and info processing styles?
- **T**: TIME MANAGEMENT - How do you effectively manage your time and schedule?

This tool can be used during onboarding, team meetings, or performance reviews. When I work with teams on creating cultures of neuroinclusion, I introduce the Respect Rubric and explore the questions as a group as a team building exercise.

None of the questions ask about a diagnosis (diagnosis and disclosure intersect with privilege). This is an opportunity for neurodivergent and disabled employees to talk about their access, support, and sensory needs without fear of negative consequences. Tools are only neuroinclusive when both neurodivergent and neurotypical people can access them and feel safe engaging with them.

27

Framework Summarized

In case you are one of those people who skips to the final chapters to seek summaries and conclusions rather than reading the entire book, I have something for you. First, you may want to consider ADHD (haha).

Second, I offer you this summarized Ask-Affirm-Accommodate-Advocate Framework:

- **ASK:** Regularly seek input from all employees, including those that identify as neurodivergent or disabled, about their access and support needs and provide psychologically safe space for feedback. Always ask the person (ATP) how they identify. Do not make assumptions.
- **AFFIRM:** Believe and validate lived experiences, identities, and needs. Honor intersectionality. Be neurodiversity AND LGBTQIA+ affirming. Drop the "D" for disorder from your vocabulary. Prioritize peopling and treating all minds and bodies with care and respect.
- **ACCOMMODATE:** Using inclusive design tools, proactively provide support that meets the access and support needs of employees without requiring formal diagnosis or disclosure, remembering how those intersect with privilege. Offer ERG's, mental health support, and coaching.
- **ADVOCATE:** Take action to address the needs of people at work. Stand up for their human rights. Prioritize accessibility. Speak up if you notice

microaggressions, bullying, and harassment. Help to rectify inequities and injustices by sharing necessary paradigm shifts. Hire people (like me:) to offer continued training and support.

Implementing this framework, you are creating a more neuroinclusive and accessible workplace—you are unlocking the full potential of your entire workforce and building a more successful organization that will meet the needs of future generations.

Thirdly, I have included a visual layout of my Neuroinclusion Framework Summary in Part Two. This is a good tool to print out and reference quickly.

This is not charitable work; this is dutiful work.

We are all interconnected and share responsibility in creating and sustaining cultures. Helping each other is not simply being kind and generous, it is accepting our moral obligation as humans. Creating cultures of neuroinclusion is good for business and good for humanity. Win, win!

28

Trailblazers and Resources

Several organizations are emerging as trailblazers and leaders in neuroinclusion and accessibility. I want to recognize the people and places that are peopling well! Other than JP MorganChase, I have personal and positive experience working with all of the other organizations on this list.

Discover Financial Services

Discover earns a top score on the Disability Equality Index. Discover has earned a 100 score on the Disability Equality Index and been recognized as a 2024 Best Place to Work for People with Disabilities. The Disability Equality Index is a comprehensive benchmarking tool to measure disability workplace inclusion inside Fortune 1000 companies. Special shout out for Discover's "Spill the Tea" film series which highlighted navigating finances with ADHD and autism. I was hired as their "neurodiversity expert and advocate" and I couldn't have been more impressed.

https://www.discover.com/

TBWA\Chiat\Day

AKA "The Disruption Company" develops strategies, advertising, and creative content for some of the world's most iconic brands. I cannot say enough about how this company excels in neuroinclusion and peopling. I worked with them on and off set for a collaboration with Omnicom Production, Lucky Twins Films, and Discover Financial Services "Spill the Tea" film series. I was continuously impressed with their efforts to include, accommodate, and affirm their employees and collaborators.
https://www.tbwachiatday.com/

Deloitte

Created structured programs that emphasize neurodiversity and the prevention of "group think" by encouraging cognitive diversity. The company values the unique perspectives that neurodivergent employees bring—leveraging their problem-solving skills to reduce homogeneity in teams, which in turn leads to innovative solutions.
https://www2.deloitte.com

Microsoft

Known for pioneering neuroinclusion, particularly through its hiring and workplace adaptation initiatives for neurodivergent employees. The company's Neurodiversity Hiring Program actively recruits individuals with autism and other neurodivergent conditions. Microsoft's inclusive design approach allows employees to contribute to a welcoming work culture that benefits everyone involved.
https://www.microsoft.com

Disability:In

An amazing resource! They are the leading nonprofit resource for business disability inclusion worldwide.
https://disabilityin.org

IBM

An accessibility pioneer, actively designing technology for inclusivity since 1914. The company's Disability ERG promotes employment for individuals with disabilities and supports accessible work environments through its technology solutions and adaptive software. IBM's dedication is grounded in historical practices and is also reflected in its talent pipeline programs aimed at hiring and training people with disabilities.
https://www.ibm.com

JPMorganChase

Recognized for its comprehensive neuroinclusion initiative, particularly through its Autism at Work program, which began in 2015. This program focuses on recruiting, supporting, and retaining neurodivergent individuals. Their Business Solution Team (BEST) promotes neuroincluion on a global scale.
https://www.jpmorganchase.com/

A BIG shout out to the place where I snuggled in to write this book:

Novel

A book bar, and cafe in my hometown of Portland, Maine. This place is a gem! It is neuroinclusive and disability inclusive. There is an elevator that leads patrons to accessible gender-neutral bathrooms and a variety of different seating options from comfy couches in cozy corners to bar stools at a large window for people watching.

The walls are covered in bookshelves and colorful art. They keep the music volume low and the spirits high. Surround yourself with other neurodivergent, disabled, and queer people while enjoying delicious food and drink and creative community events. I'll meet you for a coffee when you come to visit!
https://www.novelmaine.com/

Books on neurodiversity and disability that I highly recommend and LOVE:

Neuroqueer Heresies: Notes on the Neurodiversity Paradigm, Autistic Empowerment, and Postnormal Possibilities by Dr. Nick Walker
https://neuroqueer.com/neuroqueer-heresies/

The Canary Code: A guide to neurodiversity, dignity, and intersectional belonging at work by Ludmilla N. Praslova, PhD
https://thecanarycode.com/

We Are All Neurodiverse by Sonny Jane Wise
https://www.livedexperienceeducator.com/

The Neurodiversity Edge: The Essential Guide to Embracing Autism, ADHD, Dyslexia, and Other Neurotypes at Work by Maureen Dunne
https://www.theneurodiversityedge.org/

Demystifying Disability: What to Know, What to Say, and How to be an Ally by Emily Ladau
https://emilyladau.com/book/

Creating Cultures of Neuroinclusion: A Framework for Peopling and Engaging Neurodiverse Talent by Pasha Marlowe (I had to do it!)
https://pashamarlowe.com/

Please reach out with questions or for extra support. I offer keynotes, workshops, consulting, and coaching. I would love to see how my offerings meet your needs.

There are many ways to reach me and learn more about my work:

- Website https://pashamarlowe.com/
- Email pasha@pashamarlowe.com
- Linkedin https://www.linkedin.com/in/pashamarlowe/

Thank you for caring about neuroinclusion. Happy Peopling!

II

Part Two

29

Neuroinclusion Framework Summary

This section contains a summary of the Neuroinclusion Framework—a visual guide for creating spaces where all people, regardless of their neurological or physical differences, can thrive.

Peopling is more than a skill; it is a practice of intentional care and kindness. It is about building cultures that honor diverse ways of thinking, moving, and being. This framework highlights key practices of neuroinclusion, focusing on "peopling" through respect, empathy, and inclusion. It supports those who incorporate neuroinclusion into their interactions, work, and community spaces.

How to Use This Framework

- **Print for Reference**: Keep a copy nearby as a daily reminder.
- **Frame It**: Display it in your workspace as a commitment to inclusivity.
- **Post in Shared Spaces**: Hang it in common areas to foster a culture of kindness.
- **Share with Colleagues**: Distribute to those who may benefit from neuroinclusion practices.

For a downloadable copy, visit www.pashamarlowe.com.

CREATING CULTURES OF NEUROINCLUSION

NEUROINCLUSION is...
Engaging everyone
Peopling respectfully
Designing for accessibility
Shifting paradigms
Valuing intersectionality
Creating sustainable growth

Creating Cultures of **Neuroinclusion**
PASHA MARLOWE, MFT

QR code-30 min consultation with Pasha

01. NEUROINCLUSION
Neuroinclusion is the practice of including everyone, neurodivergent and neurotypical alike. It is about specifically creating an environment that **values and accommodates all neurological functioning styles** (thinking, feeling, moving).

02. PEOPLING
Peopling is **the practice of caring for people** with respect and kindness, affirming identities, supporting access needs, valuing unique and authentic ways of functioning, and holding empathetic space for differences and opposing views.

03. NEURODIVERSITY
The concept that neurological differences are a normal part of human variation. Neurodiversity is about the diversity of all human minds and ways of functioning. **We are all neurodiverse.** There are no neurodiverse individuals.

04. NEURODIVERGENT
An individual whose neurobiological function **diverges from neuronormativity,** or society's idea of what is "normal", "right", or "ideal". Neurodivergent is an identity, not a diagnosis. Neurodivergence includes FAR more than ADHD/VAST, autism, and dyslexia-there are hundreds of ways to diverge!

05. PARADIGM SHIFTS
The neurodiversity paradigm, in opposition to the pathology paradigm, states that human minds can respond in various ways, each person unique with their own strengths and challenges. This perspective reframes these challenges as **differences rather than deficits or disorders.**

06. BUSINESS CASE
Increased innovation, problem solving, productivity, adaptability, collaboration, and sustainable growth. With enthusiastic engagement comes less stagnation, turnover, and unnecessary conflict. Neuroinclusive workplaces have shown **90% increased retention rates.**

07. FUTURE OF WORK
1/2 of Gen Z and 1/3 of Millennials identify as **neurodivergent and disabled** (apparent and non-apparent disability). Up to 70% of neurodivergent people identify as LGBTQIA+. The future of work is more diverse and neuroqueer than ever!

08. INCLUSIVE LANGUAGE
*There are no diverse or neurodiverse individuals
*High/low functioning societies, not people
*Superpower or Disability? Yes, And.
*Accessible, not handicapped parking/bathrooms
*Drop the "D" for disorder and ATP!

09. ASK THE PERSON
Remember, Ask The Person (ATP) how they identify and what their access, sensory, and support needs are. **Do not make assumptions** based on other neurodivergent or disabled people you know or on what you see. Have a conversation.

10. ND-AFFIRMING
Challenge stigma and biases
Hold people accountable to discrimination/bullying
Design inclusively to support access needs
Value agency and autonomy
Honor intersectionality and lived experience

11. INTERSECTIONALITY
Recognize how various biological, social, and cultural categories of identity interact on multiple and simultaneous levels. **Neurodiversity and disability** intersect with various other identities, magnifying the complexity of lived experiences and oppression.

12. INCLUSIVE DESIGN
At the heart of inclusive design is the **"Solve for One, Serve Many"** principle, suggesting that by designing solutions for individuals with specific access and support needs, we create innovations and systems that benefit a much wider group.

THINKING ABOUT DIFFERENCES *Differently*

13. RESPECT RUBRIC
R: RECOGNITION/FEEDBACK
E: ENVIRONMENT
S: SUPPORT
P: PRODUCTIVITY
E: ENERGY
C: COMMUNICATION
T: TIME MANAGEMENT

*Neuroinclusive questions lead to neuroinclusive policies

Let's stay connected!
pashamarlowe.com
pasha@pashamarlowe.com
Linkedin @PashaMarlowe
IG/TT @neuroqueercoach

Neuroinclusion Framework Summary

30

Glossary of Terms

- **Ableism:** A prejudiced attitude to ward disabled or neurodivergent people where value is placed on people's bodies and minds based on constructed societal norms.
- **Accessibility:** The ability to access a space, system, or entity
- **AuDHD:** Autism and ADHD
- **Intersectionality:** Coined by Kimberle Crenshaw, the notion that understanding systems of oppression and discrimination must consider multiple intersecting factors and identities.
- **Masking:** The process by which neurodivergent individuals hide or suppress their innate traits to stay safe or fit in with neurotypical expectations. While masking is physically and emotionally exhausting, it should be noted that masking is not "wrong" and does, in fact, keep people safe or open to opportunities such as jobs.
- **Multiply-neurodivergent:** Individuals who identify with multiple forms of neurodivergence.
- **Neuro:** Relating to the nervous system, which includes the brain.
- **Neurodivergence:** The state of being neurodivergent. Whether neurodivergence is innate, acquired, or developed or how someone comes to diverge is less important than the fact that some people do diverge.
- **Neurodivergent:** Referring to an individual whose neurobiological func-

tion diverges from neuronormativity, or society's idea of what is "normal," "right," or "ideal." Neurodivergent is an identity, not a diagnosis, and those that identify reject the label of "disorder" to define their differences. Even if the neurodivergent person masks or appears neurotypical, they can still identify as neurodivergent.
- **Neurodiverse:** Describing a group that includes various neurological types. An individual cannot be neurodiverse. An individual can be neurodivergent or neurotypical.
- **Neurodiversity:** The concept that neurological differences are a normal part of human variation. Neurodiversity is about the diversity of all human minds and ways of functioning.
- **Neurodiversity Paradigm:** An affirming and non-pathologizing perspective on neurodiversity that states that there is no one "normal" or "right" way to function, just as there is no one "normal" or "right" ethnicity, gender, or culture.
- **Neuroinclusion:** When all neurotypes, all minds and bodies, are included and can work together in harmony. Where all people are respected, no matter their neuro-functioning levels or support needs, all minds and bodies have equitable opportunities to thrive.
- **Neuronormativity:** Society's standard of what is "normal," "right," or "ideal."
- **Neurotypical:** Describing individuals whose function aligns with neuronormativity, or what society considers "normal," "right," or "ideal." Some define neurotypical as one who has the privilege of functioning in alignment with neuronormativity.

III

Part Three

Afterword

The final edits of this book coincided with the 2024 US election where Donald Trump was re-elected. Like many citizens around the world, I am concerned about the future of our planet. I am immediately concerned for women, immigrants, LGBTQIA+ people, disabled people, people affected by war, and Black, Brown, and Indigenous people who continue to be underrepresented, discriminated against, and harmed.

Daily advocacy work is exhausting and hard. On election night, I thought maybe I was too soft to continue this work, but I believe we need soft skills in hard times. I believe we need to listen to and care for each other better. I believe we need to learn to hold space for differences and opposing views. We don't understand each other and our divisiveness is growing. We need to learn "how to people" in order to coexist. This is the only path to peace and unity.

About the Author

Pasha Marlowe(she/they) is a marriage and family therapist, neurodivergent relationship coach, and the leading global speaker on neuroinclusion. She is best known for her intergenerational leadership work and keynotes on "Creating Cultures of Neuroinclusion" and "How to People." Pasha has been an advocate for the neurodivergent community for the past 32 years, as her passion has always been to create spaces of inclusion and belonging where all minds and bodies feel welcome.

She is the host of the "Neuroqueering" and "Neuroinclusion" podcasts and is in the process of contributing to a book by Dr. Nick Walker, who developed the concept of neuroqueering and inspired much of their work. Pasha identifies as a late in life discovered queer, autistic, ADHDer and currently lives in Maine with her partner, youngest of three children, and two doodles.

You can connect with me on:
- https://pashamarlowe.com
- https://www.linkedin.com/in/pashamarlowe
- https://www.instagram.com/neuroqueercoach
- https://www.tiktok.com/@neuroqueercoach

Made in the USA
Las Vegas, NV
26 December 2024